Leadership and SEN

Meeting the Challenge in Special and Mainstream Settings

Nick Burnett

 David Fulton Publishers

David Fulton Publishers Ltd
The Chiswick Centre, 414 Chiswick High Road, London W4 5TF

www.fultonpublishers.co.uk

First published in Great Britain by David Fulton Publishers 2005

10 9 8 7 6 5 4 3 2 1

David Fulton Publishers is a division of Granada Learning Limited, part of ITV plc.

Note: The right of Nick Burnett to be identified as the author of this work has been asserted by him in accordance with the Copyright, Designs and Patents Act 1988.

British Library Cataloguing in Publication Data
A catalogue record for this book is available from the British Library.

ISBN 1–84312–285–5

Typeset by FiSH Books, London
Printed and bound in Great Britain

Contents

About the author

Nick Burnett, during his tenure as head teacher of Addington School, was identified as 'an excellent leader' by Ofsted. This book was written as a development from his time as a Research Associate with the National College for School Leadership. Nick recently moved to Australia with his wife Clare and children Katie and Sam. He is now Managing Director of i-for-k, based in Brisbane. i-for-k is committed to developing capacity at state, district and local level in the areas of leadership, management, behaviour and increasing access through a range of strategic partnerships.

For more details please contact nick@i-for-k.com.au or visit www.i-for-k.com.au

For more details on the Research Associate programme please visit: www.ncsl.org.uk

Acknowledgements

First I would like to thank the National College for School Leadership, particularly Dr Martin Coles, for granting me a Research Associateship with them. The funding and support this provided enabled me to complete my Research Associate report 'Special Leadership'.

For more information on the Research Associates initiative please visit www.ncsl.org.uk

I would also like to thank the Governors of Addington School for allowing me, during my time as Head, to undertake my Research Associateship. Particular thanks go to my deputies Ian Ayre and Liz Meek (now Head) for not only 'holding the fort' but also continuing to lead the school in my absences. The much-deserved outcome for all the talented and dedicated staff at Addington was to be identified by Ofsted as a 'very good school with some excellent features'.

I would further like to thank the following head teachers of schools and services for so willingly giving of their time to help me with the background research for this book:

Clive Lilley – Blackfriars School
Mrs E. Jordan – Mary Elliot School
Mel Johnson – Northcott School
Chris Davies – Severndale School
Paul Donkersloot – Holyport Manor School
Ann O'Meara – Kingfisher School
Steve Cliffen – Coxlease School
Andrew Creese – Oxfordshire PRUIS
Oliver Caviglioli – seconded to Essex LEA, head teacher of SLD special school
Mike Hatch – Crosshills Technology College
Sylvia Robertshaw – Action Leeds

In Australia, thanks go to:

Roger Smailes, Principal of Castlereagh Special School, Perth
Lee Sutherland, Team Leader within Ballajura Community College, Perth
Bob Meenan, Principal of a Secondary Education Support Centre, Perth
Marlene Brown, Principal of Gladys Newton Special School, Perth
Bella Irlicht, Principal of Port Phillip Specialist School, Melbourne
Chris Forlin, Associate Professor of Edith Cowan University

Thanks also to the many successful and highly effective leaders of a range of SEN provisions whom I have been fortunate to spend some time with.

Much appreciation for their time, knowledge and expertise goes to Paul Donkersloot and Bernard Allen for reading my draft writings and providing welcome and constructive feedback.

Last, but certainly not least, a huge thankyou to my wife Clare and to my children, Katie and Sam, for their patience and understanding with me for being away from them more than usual.

Introduction

The background to the writing of this book was my time as a Research Associate with the National College for School Leadership. The focus of my research was to identify what possible implications for the leadership of special schools do potential changes to the special school system have.

The research was written from undertaking the following activities:

- Reading a wide range of current and leading-edge information on futures thinking, inclusion and the special school and identifying possible implications for the leadership of special schools
- Discussion with Focus Groups:
    ASH (Berkshire Association of Special School Heads)
    SCRIP (South Central Regional Inclusion Partnership)
- A study of practice in special schools, both on a national and international scale, and therefore linking to one of NCSL's five key research strands, 'learning from best practice worldwide'
- Interviewing heads of Beacon Special Schools – a selection of those where Leadership and Management have been identified as a strength
- Having contact with experts such as:
    Mel Ainscow
    Richard Byers
    Brian Caldwell
- Interviews with Mike Hatch (Crosshills Technology College, Blackburn) and Sylvia Robertshaw from Action Leeds, through recommendations by Mel Ainscow
- Interviews with Paul Donkersloot and Oliver Caviglioli – head teachers of special schools – through personal contacts
- International study visit to Australia:
    Perth (through recommendation by Mel Ainscow)
    Melbourne (through recommendation by Brian Caldwell)

Building on this research, this book aims to further explore the common themes that arose, along with looking at a wider range of SEN environments and recent initiatives and their possible impact. Throughout the book there are numerous examples of how a number of leaders of SEN environments are 'inventing the future'.

The book is aimed at all current and future leaders of SEN environments and should also prove a useful reference point for those involved in developing and delivering training to leaders of SEN environments. Leadership teams in all schools wishing to develop their provision for pupils with SEN will find it a stimulating read and may well benefit from further developing the case study material to consider possibilities for future developments in their own settings.

The book is structured in such a way that it can either be read from start to finish or used as a reference source through the use of the mind maps and the index. The use of mind maps is to clearly identify to the reader, at the start of each chapter, the main topics that will be covered, and then there is the opportunity to refresh these ideas and develop them further with the more detailed chapter summary mind maps. Readers can then pick out the key themes they wish to explore in a quick and easy manner.

Change

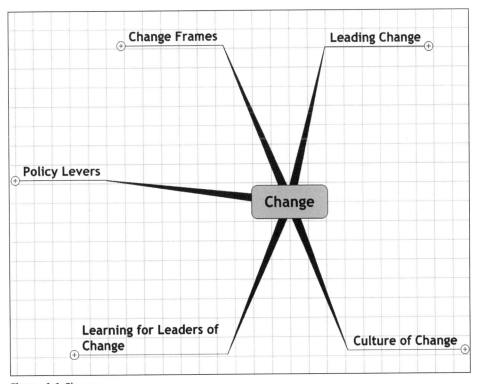

Figure 1.1 Change

> Creative thinking may mean simply the realization that there is no particular virtue in doing things the way they have always been done.
>
> (Rudolph Flesch, in McDermott 2002)

There continue to be many new and interesting initiatives that bombard school leaders in all settings in most countries across the world, but those working and leading in Special Education arenas – both special and mainstream – face a particularly radical shift in the challenges they face. With the continued debate around how to achieve inclusion and the roles, if any, of special schools in the new educational landscape, the need to invent or re-invent new ways of working has probably never been more intense. The rest of this chapter will explore what recent research has identified as being key issues for leaders in SEN fields.

The majority of leaders within SEN now recognise that the philosophical argument for inclusion is the correct one, but it is the author's experience that there remain a number who do not accept that there is a need to change and that their SEN environment is inclusive. It appears, from the author's own research, that the pace of change shows no sign of slowing and that the most effective leaders have taken this on board fully and are 'inventing the future'.

There have been numerous books and articles written about change, and elements of the mind map at the start of this chapter draw on work by a range of leading educationalists and researchers who are identified as appropriate throughout the rest of the chapter. The ideas identified will now be explored in greater detail.

Certain personal attributes are essential if the leader of SEN responsible for leading change within his/her educational establishment is to be successful. Brighouse (2002) identifies a number of qualities which, although relevant to all educational leaders, hold particular resonance for those leading in the field of SEN.

The need for *unwarranted optimism* is of great importance when faced with challenges such as: yet another review of SEN within your area; meeting the needs of a pupil with complex needs in a mainstream school; or facing a reorganisation of your school.

Also identified is the need for an attitude that sees crisis as the norm and complexity as fun. For those involved in leadership in an SEN environment this will not be particularly new and many may not see it as fun, but developing the skills, attitudes and knowledge to thrive in this environment is crucial in ensuring an efficient and effective service is provided and developed.

There has been a great deal written about the need to undertake *lifelong learning* and this remains crucial in an ever-changing environment. An endless supply of intellectual curiosity will help to ensure that decisions taken and discussions are founded on research and knowledge as well as on values and beliefs.

The last quality that Brighouse identifies as particularly relevant to those working in the special school environment is the *absence of paranoia and self-pity*. There is a great danger that those working within special environments, particularly segregated provision, feel that within the worldwide inclusion agenda there is a great deal of these emotions. As will be seen through the case studies contained within this book, the most successful leaders do not subscribe to either of these, and in many cases are leading the inclusion debate and action within the local and national arenas.

CASE STUDY

Blackfriars School

Headteacher Clive Lilley is developing Blackfriars School as a *Key Learning Centre*. He has produced a booklet which identifies clearly to staff, parents and professionals what this means in practice. Examples relevant to this section are as follows:

- To extend the knowledge and understanding of Blackfriars staff in inclusion and continue their professional development in this field through the DRIP (Developing a Resource for Inclusive Practice) Project.
- To provide a specialist outreach and support role to physically/medically impaired pupils in mainstream schools.
- To work to include all pupils for whom a place in mainstream is possible.

What has become clear is that for any leader within an SEN environment to successfully lead and create change there is the need to build capacity. Some of the key drivers to meeting this need are actively seeking to recruit staff who are energy creators rather than energy takers; ensuring opportunities to take on leadership challenges; and promoting staff welfare policies and practices. The issue of building capacity has been widely espoused within many sectors, both public and private, and key to achieving this is the ability to ensure that all stakeholders, including the teachers themselves, see teachers as leaders of change.

As was identified earlier, the quality of regarding crisis as the norm is seen as essential, and inextricably linked to this in building capacity to create change is the ability of leaders to demonstrate and build the skills of others in meeting and minimising crisis. Undoubtedly, many staff will feel threatened and challenged by crises, and therefore the really skilful leader ensures that the majority of staff feel supported and do not see issues arising as crises but are able to manage problems successfully.

The most successful leaders in SEN environments build capacity for change that:

- promotes sustained learning;
- lasts over time (involves effective succession planning);
- is supported by available resources and is achievable;
- does not impact negatively on the surrounding environment; and
- builds future capacities.

Educational change is like being on a rotten boat, with a mutinous crew, sailing into uncharted waters. Only the person not rowing has time to rock the boat.

(Prashnig 1998)

Vision is another area about which much has been written throughout the years, but the key to building capacity to create change is extending the vision. This means ensuring that the vision does not just remain the property of the senior leadership team and governors, but that all stakeholders are part of the vision, and that change drivers are clearly identified. The most effective leaders in meeting the needs of pupils with SEN ensure that all staff – teaching and support, parents and pupils – are involved in consultation during the building of the vision. These leaders have a clear vision of the future but are keen to ensure that they are in touch with all stakeholders and that they build their thoughts into the vision. What they skilfully do is to paint a picture of or tell a story about what things could be like, and they are not afraid to take people out of their comfort zones. What has also been developed is the expectation that pupils are involved in the consultation through direct questionnaires and school councils. Including pupils with communication difficulties can be a challenge but successful leaders have begun to develop systems and approaches to achieving this.

Another task identified as being important in building the capacity to create change is that of securing the environment. This means that successful leaders in SEN environments ensure that the management side of things is well established: staff handbooks are up-to-date; and policies and procedures for learning, teaching and assessment are clearly articulated, shared and understood. Looking after staff through regularly reviewing meeting schedules and making the staffroom as welcoming as possible are vital. An additional issue in many SEN environments that successful leaders have tackled in order to address the task of securing the environment is the building of teams, both small and larger, that are supportive in nature to ensure coaching/mentoring is addressed successfully and staff debriefing can happen. This is a very important process that needs to take place following incidents between staff and pupils. If staff do not feel valued and supported the capacity to create change will be greatly diminished or even non-existent.

Seeking and charting improvement is inherent within all school environments and successful leaders ensure this task is achieved. The additional challenges for leaders in many SEN environments include developing appropriate benchmarking across phases and – more difficult for those working with pupils with complex learning difficulties – across schools.

The impact of culture on change will have a significant impact and the ability of leaders within SEN environments to build a culture of change is crucial if they are to become or remain successful. The dual tasks of building capacity and creating a culture of change are something of a 'chicken-and-egg' situation; neither can be done in isolation and each has a bearing on the success of the other.

> **CASE STUDY**
> _____
>
> **Addington School**
>
> - The school has developed its own Autumn Package that contains assessment information on all pupils in all subjects over the previous three years.
> - This information is being used to chart and monitor individual progress.
> - The school, with the LEA, is developing information to assess value added in the following way: pupils are baselined and then put together as cohorts as follows:
>
>   P1–P3; P4–P8; National Curriculum Levels

Effective leaders in SEN environments are able to successfully restructure and re-culture at the same time and hence rapidly develop schools and build capacity to re-invent themselves.

Michael Fullan (2001), in his book *Leading in a Culture of Change*, identifies articulately five common themes which leaders need to develop if they are to build a culture of change. These will now be explored along with their particular relevance to leadership and SEN.

The first issue identified by Fullan is that of *moral purpose*. It is clear that there needs to be a moral purpose defining the values and beliefs of leaders within all contexts, particularly during periods of rapid and extended change. This is of particular relevance for leaders in SEN environments as they need to make decisions and lead these environments during the challenge of developing inclusion. The author believes that there is a moral imperative to make a difference that has particular relevance to those leading within SEN environments and this is seen at four levels: the individual level; the school level; beyond school; and in society.

Most of those involved in leading, teaching or working with pupils within SEN environments have a strong desire to make a difference to the individual pupil. Leaders and staff have a strong desire to make a difference at a school level, but how many look beyond school and, still more challenging, to society?

Those working within SEN environments would claim to be strong advocates of the right of the child to high-quality provision, so who better to drive forward the inclusion agenda, ensuring individual needs are met?

Fight the change or grab hold and enjoy the ride.

(Peters 2003)

The second issue identified is that of *understanding change*. The key element here is that as leaders we need to tackle the obstacles to change, and we can only be successful if we understand how change works. In the educational environment, where there can be an overload of initiatives, it is important that we play a filtering role, and in successful SEN environments leaders have achieved this through critical thinking, openness to new possibilities and an unwavering belief in what they know to be in the best interests of the pupils. They have also been assisted in that the majority of new initiatives coming forward do not have the needs of pupils with SEN at the forefront of their thinking, and therefore the successful leaders within SEN environments are able to argue effectively, even with Ofsted, for what they have, or have not, implemented. A cautionary note here is that this only tends to be successful when a robust and effective alternative has been put in place.

The next area is that of *relationships* (or as Fullan puts it, 'relationships, relationships, relationships'). It is clear that the development of effective relationships at many levels is vital if you are to be successful in leading during periods of change. The need to look at building and sustaining strategic alliances with a whole range of people is vital if as a leader you are to chart a successful path through change. It is important to note at this stage that effective leaders within SEN environments recognise their locus of influence and that, if they are to be successful, they will need to develop relationships with stakeholders who are beyond the authority of the leaders, such as political figures. There is a useful acronym to remember when dealing with all people who are stakeholders but particularly those who are outside of your control. It is CIA (Change; Influence; Accept). There are certain stakeholders whose views you will be able to change, some you will be able to influence and some you will have to accept and work with, or around.

As was identified earlier as a quality of a successful leader, the need for intellectual curiosity is very important. Fullan identifies this as *knowledge building* and this goes beyond the idea of just the leader being a lifelong learner – it explores how the leader builds structures and systems for the sharing of knowledge, which is probably one of the most important – if not the most important – elements to building a successful and effective SEN environment.

Effective knowledge building and sharing enables new practices to become embedded and shared quickly both within schools and with other educational establishments. Leaders within SEN environments are well placed to lead on this as there is often the presence of more than one adult in the classroom and so discussion and dialogue can be initiated more readily. There are always the difficulties of time and money to ensure this happens. See the case study material in Chapter 4 on 'Innovation' for examples of how some schools are trying to build their knowledge sharing capacities.

The final strand explored by Fullan is that of *coherence making*. This relates directly back to a number of the capacity building factors identified earlier in connection with extending the vision, securing the environment and seeking and charting improvement. It is vital that there is a clear vision of where the SEN environment is aiming to be, alongside developing an understanding that achieving the vision is a journey and that there is no blueprint. This is easy to say and much harder to achieve in practice. Effective leaders instil a sense of confidence in those working within these environments who are reassured, but do not follow blindly, and encouraged to debate and discuss the path and approaches taken.

In addition to the areas identified by Fullan, the following areas are also indicative of the changing cultural context in which SEN leaders are now working.

There is a growing demand to engage in intimate *consultation* with key stakeholders. Whilst many leaders have done this successfully with staff and governors, only a few have fully embraced the need to instigate and listen to the enhanced pupil voice and parental preference lobby which has continued to gain status and power over recent years. Many leaders have involved parents and, more recently, pupils in the completion of questionnaires about how they view the school, its ethos etc., but how many have engaged in truly intimate consultation about what they like, dislike or expect the school to achieve?

There are often even greater challenges to those working within SEN environments. For parents, the time their child is at school is often a time of respite for them, or they may have had negative personal educational experiences themselves. Whilst leaders need to be aware of the additional demands placed on them, there are many parents who have fought long and hard to get what they feel is right for their child and, as such, are extremely articulate at putting forward their case. Also, ensuring there is true advocacy for pupils with SEN remains a strongly debated area. There are those who would argue that the parents are best placed, but there are times when the understandably additional stresses placed on them as parents of a child with SEN may not make them the best advocates. On many occasions a school member of staff is seen as an effective advocate, but again, they may well have values and beliefs that do not match that of the child. The role of the sibling of a child with SEN is often neglected – not only their additional needs but also the possibility of them acting as an advocate for their brother or sister. It still leaves many questions, and the main responsibility of leaders in SEN environments is to try and give the individual the ability to make meaningful and informed choices for themselves.

The final area regarding changing cultural context to be initially explored is that of *partnership provision*. This will be covered in much more detail in the next chapter on partnerships but suffice to say that there has been a significant shift in the educational landscape in England to try and encourage this with the formation of Networked Learning Communities, Federations and joint Specialist School bids, although, unfortunately, the latter has been removed so that

Secondary and Special Schools can no longer submit joint applications. As will be seen through the case study material in the partnerships chapter, the most successful leaders of SEN environments worked extremely hard to develop partnerships in order to not only strengthen their own environments but also the environments they were partnering, to the benefit of all pupils and staff involved.

On a number of occasions throughout this chapter the issue of lifelong learning and knowledge building has been discussed. This will now be explored in more detail regarding the specific areas of learning for leaders of change, drawing on work by Stoll *et al.* (2004) who identified seven areas.

The first area identified is that of *understanding learning*. There have been huge strides in the past few years regarding the knowledge available to enable us to have an increased understanding of how people learn. In effective schools this is being put into practice in the SEN field and there has been some interesting developments in some schools, explored later in this book, regarding a range of initiatives to implement the research on learning styles and multiple intelligences. Herein lies the key challenge to leaders within the field of SEN: how to make the research relevant and applicable to their own individual environments. In addition to the development of effective practices within the classroom the key to building capacity within SEN environments is understanding the need to meet the learning styles of a range of staff in order to build their knowledge and capacity effectively, the key challenge being that there is usually a much wider range of adults working within SEN environments than in other environments.

The need to build coherence and understanding, both personally and for others, through making connections from the wide range of information, research and views that are available to access nowadays is vital for the successful SEN leader. Through this he/she will be able to chart a coherent path through the individual environment which is unique to each setting, and hence the need for a high level of contextual knowledge. Without a secure understanding of the unique situation and factors that influence each environment sustained improvement will not be achieved.

Closely linked to this is the ability to use critical thinking. While this can, and on occasion needs to, be done in isolation, usually the most effective method is for this to be undertaken by the leadership team or whoever is best placed to contribute. The ability to undertake truly effective critical thinking is not always as easy as is believed, and tools such as De Bono's 'Thinking Caps' have been trialled by some schools to help develop this skill.

Another area identified by Stoll *et al.* is that of *political acumen*. As was identified earlier, the effective leader of an SEN environment needs to know and understand who they can change, influence or accept (CIA), but this can only be achieved with a good knowledge of what the drivers and motivators are for those working within the political arena. Time spent learning about this area can prove very useful and can save a lot of time in achieving desired aims and goals. The area of SEN can prove to be a very powerful one when used carefully within the political arena.

Allied to the political acumen area of learning, but certainly not exclusively, is that of *emotional understanding*. Again, a great deal of research has been undertaken in respect of emotional literacy and emotional intelligence that has particular resonance for those working within the SEN field. An enhanced knowledge of the area of emotional understanding will help develop competencies and skills in working with pupils with SEN and also – directly linked to what Stoll *et al.* are referring to – working with adults. As stated, this is important learning to undertake if you are to understand the motivators of those working within the political field, and also other stakeholders. In addition, more than one of the effective leaders interviewed as part of the research for this book spoke about the need to actively recruit the 'right sort of person', and when this was explored in more detail it emerged that they were referring to those with high levels of emotional intelligence.

If you don't like change, you're going to like irrelevance even less.

(General Eric Shinseki, Chief of Staff in US Army, quoted in Peters 2003)

The last area identified by Stoll *et al.* as important learning for leaders of change is in the area of *futures thinking*. Case study material explores the way that a number of the successful leaders in SEN environments were involved in futures thinking particularly with regard to strategic planning. Beare (1996) summarised the importance of crystal ball gazing clearly by identifying three types of futures:

- *Possible futures* – things which *could* happen, although many are unlikely;
- *Probable futures* – things which probably *will* happen unless something is done to turn events around; and
- *Preferable futures* – things which you would *prefer* to happen and which you plan to make happen.

In the third type, leaders bring their own values and beliefs to the fore and it is important to have been developing all the other areas of learning to ensure this is context-specific, relevant and up-to-date, as this may well involve changing or adapting long-held beliefs and attitudes.

In building capacity within schools, including the ability to meet the need for change, it is important to recognise the use of policy levers to bring about school and authority-/district-wide change. Leaders, as has been explored throughout this chapter, play a pivotal role in both providing within school and demanding from the LEA the necessary policy levers to bring about the change they desire within their SEN environments. The need for intense professional development to support the change is vital in sustaining and developing change that has been implemented, and alongside this is the need for ongoing monitoring.

As much as the need for monitoring may not seem to be welcomed by many, it is crucial in ensuring that gains made do not disappear once the spotlight has moved to the next area of change. This monitoring obviously needs to involve internal mechanisms but also benefits from external monitoring – by Ofsted or the like – to ensure that gains have been truly made and for the collection of hard and soft data as to *how* these gains have been made, with clear outcomes.

CASE STUDIES

Mary Elliot School

Headteacher Mrs E. Jordan is currently providing:

- Staff training with the intention that all staff feel comfortable in offering outreach or working in mainstream schools; and
- Work shadowing – a two-way arrangement with mainstream colleagues spending time in the special school and special school staff spending time in the mainstream school.

Essex LEA

Oliver Caviglioli, Head of an SLD school on a part-time secondment working for the LEA, is developing the idea of:

- 'Pathfinder' schools to be established to try out the new ideas and approaches.

In order to achieve all of the above, there needs to be developed a high level of relational trust. This needs to have been developed through the building of the culture/climate and through respect and personal regard for others displayed to both adults and pupils within the SEN environment, certainly by the leaders and preferably by all those involved. It is also built through the demonstration of competence and integrity, by being prepared to do anything you are asking of others to a high level and by being true to your values and beliefs in your actions as well as your words.

The development of relational trust often takes time within the SEN environment but the effective leader can build this through his/her actions and responses. The greater challenge for both the SEN leader and the relevant external stakeholders is to build this relational trust to assist in system-wide change and transformation being achieved.

In such a complex ever-changing environment within which SEN leaders are working it is important to use available tools to help make sense of that environment and to ensure that nothing gets overlooked. A useful concept developed by Hargreaves *et al.* (2000) is that of change frames, which enable schools to look at change through multiple lenses to ensure that the school asks more informed questions of the changes they are facing. The seven frames are:

- Purpose
- Emotional
- Political
- Cultural
- Structural
- Leadership
- Organisational and professional learning

As can be seen, these cover many of the areas discussed in more detail earlier in the chapter. (Readers wishing to know more about the development and use of change frames can refer to the References and Further Reading section for the relevant reference.)

The following approach to leadership, though meant to be humorous, highlights many of the issues faced by leaders involved in change environments, and was drawn from a presentation on the '21st Century School' by Steve Kenning, Research Associate and Head Teacher, Callington Community School, Cornwall. In the presentation, Kenning identified that he had read an article where a comparison between surfing and management had been developed using the following analogies:

- Passion rules
- No dare, no flair
- Expect to wipe out
- Don't turn your back on the ocean
- Keep looking outside
- Move before it moves you
- Never surf alone

I am sure that leaders within SEN establishments will agree with many of these sentiments!

Summary

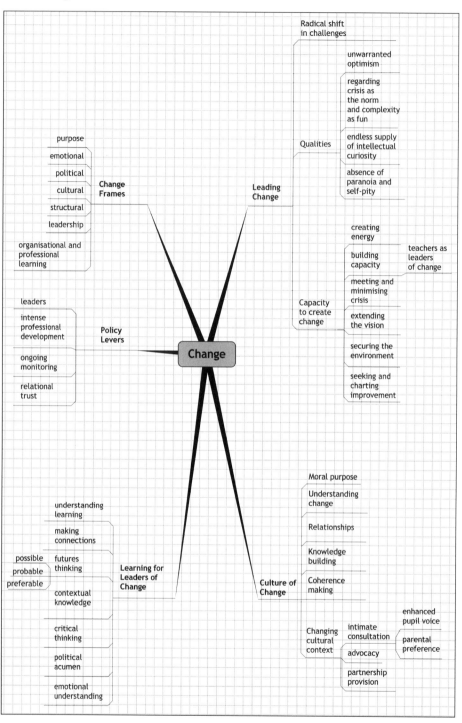

Figure 1.2 Change summary

CHAPTER 2

Partnerships

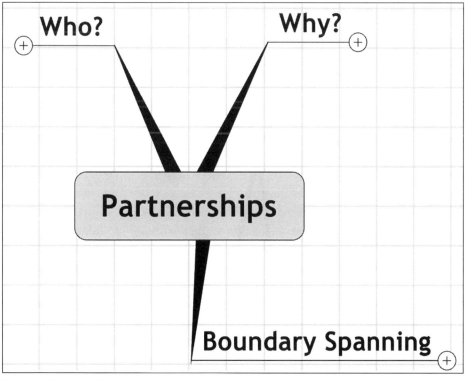

Figure 2.1 Partnerships

I found the development of successful partnerships to be a common theme when visiting successful SEN environments and talking with their leaders. Despite this it is always important to use critical thinking to assess whether it is such a crucial area or just a coincidence.

From discussion with leaders in a range of SEN environments, and from reading, there appears to be a number of factors as to why successful leaders in SEN environments seek to build partnerships.

The first one that will be explored is that of *support*. It was clear that although the SEN environment that was seeking the partnership had a great deal to offer a range of partners, this was most certainly not the only motive; they believed that their staff and pupils would also gain a great deal. It was also felt that the partnership would bring a greater opportunity for staff and pupils from both environments to experience diversity. The fact that staff and pupils from the SEN and mainstream environments would be joining together would assist in breaking down barriers that had built up over the many years of segregated provision. Pupils from the SEN environments would have opportunities to mix with a wider range of peers and, hopefully, experience more 'normalised' behaviour, while the pupils from the mainstream environment would get to interact with the full range of peers they had within their community. For staff from the SEN environment there would be the opportunity to see what is expected, behaviourally and academically, of pupils in the mainstream settings; for staff from the mainstream environment they would have the opportunity to interact with a diverse range of pupils as well as, hopefully, the opportunity to share and gain strategies for meeting the needs of SEN pupils within their own setting.

Through the development of these strategic partnerships there is a greater opportunity to offer support and diversity in terms of meeting the needs of pupils with special needs in both settings. Strategic successful leaders were often able to access a wider range of additional funding. While it was not a major driver for the initiation of the partnerships, the possibility of additional funding aided their development in a number of cases. The most astute of the SEN leaders were adept at spotting financial opportunities to benefit their environments' development further as well as aiding partners.

With a strong and successful partnership it would appear that there develops an enhanced *productivity* which builds capacity within each organisation to meet their designated vision and aims, particularly for those pupils with SEN. It is not by accident that this happens or without support and encouragement from leaders in both settings; the stronger the partnership, as in the case of most co-located or satellite provisions, the greater the productivity and ability to meet the needs of the pupils with SEN. The more interactions that take place between pupils and staff from both environments, the less the barriers are evident, but it is clear that it is possible to have very segregated provision on the same site if the structures and systems do not support interaction as well as, most importantly, the beliefs and values of the leaders.

Closely linked to the area of increased productivity is that of *service delivery*. Service delivery – the educational establishment's ability to meet its primary

---

CASE STUDY

Blackfriars School

The school is:

- offering a pre-school scheme for special needs pupils with the aim of integrating these pupils into local mainstream provision by statutory school age. It is called BEARS (Blackfriars Education and Access Resource Scheme);

- working in collaboration with local FE colleges to develop and extend the school's 16–19 work as an inclusive FE provider with funding from the Learning and Skills Council;

- extending the Home–School Partnership to include parents and pupils with special needs in mainstream schools;

- providing a linked relationship with named schools and colleges to provide pupils with mainstream experience and social inclusion;

- providing professional development support for teachers and teaching assistants in mainstream schools to increase their capacity to support inclusion.

---

purpose, i.e. high-quality education for the pupils within it – is likely to be more effective as the educational opportunities on offer will be extended with the wider range of partnerships established.

Another reason that was given by leaders of SEN environments for developing partnerships was the ability to *share on a range of levels*. While there is a lot of rhetoric regarding an increased level of trust between government and schools, there is, not surprisingly, still a lot of reticence to be involved in activities that are seen as risky. When involved in partnership development a key element identified was that the risk was shared through a joint approach. More important was that there was an increased opportunity for creativity given that there were more people involved in brainstorming thoughts and ideas. Again, the level of creativity and risk depended very much on the ethos and atmosphere generated by the leaders in the partnership environments. There needs to be a clearly shared understanding of what is acceptable from both leaders if a truly creative environment is to be fostered, and staff and pupils must feel trusted to work within agreed parameters. The most effective examples were when staff and pupils were expected to push back the boundaries of what was often felt possible.

Alongside the sharing of risk and creativity is the sharing of *responsibility*. This has a number of meanings and is certainly not restricted to the responsibility for risk and creativity. An additional meaning that was evident from discussions was that the development of partnerships was about fostering

CASE STUDIES

Severndale School is providing:

● outreach support;

● a teacher training base – setting up Management Modules in Partnership with HE.

Crosshills Technology College has:

● a school target of ensuring that every pupil spends some time in mainstream;

● an Inclusion Project with a 0.7 fte Inclusion Co-ordinator and a full-time teaching assistant;

● team teaching with a mainstream school;

● a plan to move mainstream teachers into the special school and vice versa.

responsibility for all pupils within the partners' communities and about building capacity to be more effective at meeting their needs.

The last area of sharing that has been identified is that of *resources*. Leaders of SEN environments recognised that they had access to a wide range of resources that would be beneficial to those working within mainstream environments as well. Not only did they share access to specialist classroom resources, including ICT and areas such as multi-sensory rooms and hydrotherapy pools, but, more importantly, they found ways to share their most important resource, their staff. There is a huge amount of knowledge, skills and expertise within the SEN environment and the effective SEN leader finds ways of sharing partnerships while ensuring that the provision does not suffer. Some of this has already been identified earlier when discussing the benefits for both sets of pupils and staff involved in partnership arrangements but it does require strong leadership to ensure all staff and parents see that the benefits will outweigh the difficulties.

It appears from the recent literature and discussions with highly effective leaders of SEN environments that it is increasingly important that leaders look toward 'boundary spanning'. By this is meant the ability to work across what many would see as normal boundaries. For leaders in SEN environments this means especially between education, health and social services. To do this successfully the leader needs to understand the other sectors' limitations and constraints, while establishing positive relationships for all involved.

As we enter the 21st century, it is more important than ever to provide comprehensive and integrated educational, mental health, medical and social interventions. Full-service schools represent a convenient way for students and their families to access these services.

(Swerdlik et al. 1999)

The full-service school concept has been embraced by a number of schools in the USA, and it seems to have particular relevance for leaders of SEN environments as the majority of the pupils within these environments have involvement with either social services or health, and in many cases both. While the concept of the Extended School, currently being developed in England, is a significant step forward, it would seem that leaders of SEN environments are well down the list of schools likely to be granted this status, despite their providing for a significant number of vulnerable children.

While attaining Extended School status may seem a distant dream to many leaders in SEN environments, boundary spanning is more easily attainable, and is currently being developed in various contexts. Many leaders of SEN environments have already established good links with the health authorities and social services and are building on these to help provide a more holistic approach to meeting the needs of the pupils. The most effective SEN environments already have a close partnership with multidisciplinary teams which includes health and social services professionals. The boundary spanning leader will be successful if he/she can establish a model based on interdependence, collaboration and enlightened self-interest.

The full-service school takes boundary spanning a step further by providing a co-ordinated 'wraparound' package to the 'client', the pupil and the parents, by having all associated professionals working in a holistic way, in partnership, on the same site.

Who do the leaders of SEN environments partner with in addition to those mentioned earlier? From the case study material contained within this chapter, and throughout the book, it can be seen that many effective leaders of SEN environments partner with a wide range of establishments.

Most obviously, they link with *other schools*, and the partnership arrangements vary from loose links for occasional pupils through to co-location on the same site with joint staffing appointments. The common thread for leaders of SEN environments is the desire of the most effective leaders to make this happen. They will spend a lot of time, in and out of school, promoting the opportunities and rewarding, through a variety of means, those staff and other schools who are willing to take the risk. They celebrate each small achievement with staff, parents, pupils and external stakeholders to encourage further possibilities. They also look for, and take advantage of, any possibilities and are not overly concerned with the motives of others.

CASE STUDY

Leeds LEA has:

- partnership schools – groups of pupils go with teachers, teaching assistants and resources into mainstream schools;
- shared planning time between special school and mainstream teachers of a minimum of half a day per half-term;
- the aim of 50 per cent of SEN pupils based in partnership schools with the remaining 50 per cent having some inclusion opportunities;
- discussions with the Health Authority to develop a Health Audit for pupils in special schools.

The Specialist School status that is available to all secondary schools, and special schools with secondary-aged pupils, is one such possibility for many leaders of SEN environments, although it is recognised that this is easier for some SEN environments than others, particularly those working with pupils with SEBD. These additional or different challenges are covered in Chapter 5. The key issues that the Specialist School must address are: to develop and support partnerships with other schools and with the community. Within the other schools is the necessity to foster a partnership with a special school, and it is here that many possibilities (often built on the desire for the additional funding) for partnerships with mainstream schools occur. Effective leaders of SEN environments use this to their advantage and build from this first stepping stone. A number of successful leaders have also taken advantage of the loophole which allows special schools to apply for specialist status to actively seek additional partnerships with the added bonus of additional funding. As mentioned earlier, it is still a mystery as to why the opportunity to put in joint bids between secondary and special schools was recently removed, as this, with its additional funding, was often an initial driver for a number of inclusive partnerships.

Building partnerships with the *local community and with industry* is also seen by many effective leaders as a crucial aspect to the development of their environment. Again the challenges faced by the different SEN environments will be covered later, but those who have been able to succeed have done so in a range of innovative ways. These include developing the community aspect of a specialist bid; and exploring how they can assist in further developing provision for those within the community, including the elderly and also adults with SEN. Many have also fostered and encouraged close links with local community facilities such as libraries, as this extends the provision they are able to offer as well as reducing some of the 'fear' associated with meeting pupils with SEN.

The links with industry have brought benefits for pupils, staff and the industries themselves. Pupils have been given opportunities to undertake work experience, training in CV writing and interview skills to name a few. For staff there is the possibility of industry placements, access to meeting facilities and, in the case of the author, a highly successful and influential mentoring arrangement with a senior human resource manager in a local company (see below).

CASE STUDY

Addington School has:

- an outreach support role developed through:
  telephone and e-mail helplines;
  teacher and TA support visits to mainstream schools and also into Addington;
- Support Teachers involved in delivering LEA school training in the areas of:
  ICT
  Behaviour
  Autistic Spectrum Disorder;
- developed a Partnership Schools Project to encourage more inclusion opportunities for staff and pupils with mainstream schools leading to a Gifted and Talented group of students from a local secondary school working with a group of peers with PMLD to create accessible musical instruments;
- established a mentoring partnership with a senior human resource manager giving the following benefits:
  opportunities to gain a non-educational view;
  access to external facilitators looking at staff communication issues.

The partnerships with para-professionals has already been covered to some extent within this chapter but an additional note for leaders of SEN environments is that those who have been most successful ensure that they are fully included within the structure and systems of the environment and not seen as an add-on. It has also been noted that, although there is some resistance from some professions, the most effective provision is where these professionals operate within classrooms for the majority of their time. This helps reduce barriers to understanding between the different professionals, and means of provision is more 'joined up'.

It may seem odd to talk about a partnership with *parents* as this forms part of nearly all school environment aims, but it is worth noting the possible specific challenges faced by the leader of the SEN environment. As has been noted earlier, the additional pressures faced by parents of pupils with SEN should never be underestimated, and as such, successful leaders are aware of what support they can ask for and offer to assist. They recognise that parents have a unique knowledge of the pupil and foster appropriate strategies to support them wherever possible. The development of parent training programmes in a range of strategies used across the school helps to ensure a consistent approach is developed in dealing with pupils with SEN across the different environments they experience. A note of caution must be sounded in that it can be difficult and/or stressful for many parents to come into schools, so alternative venues and approaches should be sought where possible.

The final group to be looked at with regard to partnerships is that of *voluntary organisations.* This is an area that is virtually unique to those working within the SEN sector and will vary significantly from one SEN sector to another and from one area to another. As one successful leader succinctly identified, there is the need for a very clear procedure regarding the professional conduct and relationships to be shared and agreed between all parties if a productive working relationship is to be developed. It is recognised that voluntary organisations play a very important role in assisting and supporting individuals with SEN and their families, but they may also have a particular belief that may put them in conflict with the educational establishment and its leaders.

Summary

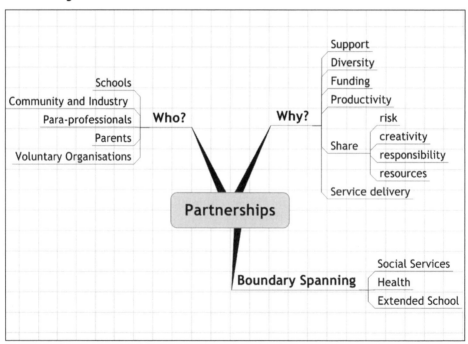

Figure 2.2 Partnerships summary

CHAPTER 3

ICT

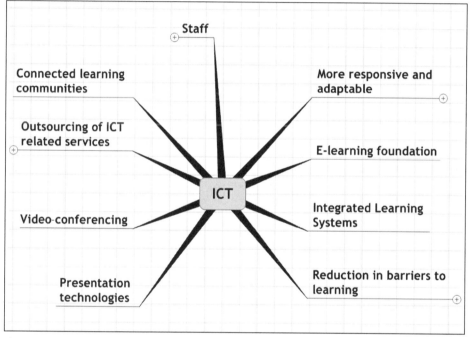

Figure 3.1 ICT

The school of the future is going to rely on people with a vision to enhance the skills and learning of everyone. (a primary school teacher quoted in *Transforming the Way We Learn* (DfES 2002b)

There are no doubt a number of you reading this book who are far from convinced about the projected impact of ICT espoused by many, and particularly within the SEN environments in which you lead and work, but you would be hard pressed not to accept that there have been significant changes during the past 5–10 years, and it is likely that these will continue. Whether we get to the position of the virtual school for pupils without learning difficulties is highly debatable and few would suggest that it is a useful way forward for those with more complex learning difficulties. In spite of all the doubts, ICT has been given the status of a separate chapter within this book because of the profound effects it has had on the SEN education landscape for the majority of pupils and staff. The key areas arising out of the recent literature, and from the discussions with highly effective leaders of SEN environments, will now be explored.

The development of technology that is more responsive and adaptable to learner needs has significant implications for pupils of all abilities being able to take greater control of their learning through the appropriate and effective application of ICT.

The technologies continue to evolve to provide increased functionality and greater portability, and the software applications are becoming more intelligent and responsive to the user. These developments are providing exciting opportunities for pupils to personalise their access to digital learning resources in and out of school. This is likely to become increasingly important for pupils with special needs or medical conditions that may prevent them from attending regular classes. Pupils are now able to communicate through a myriad of different devices and it is quite likely that a number are only limited by our expertise, knowledge, problem-solving and the prohibitive cost of some technology. It is equally likely that as technology continues to develop at such a pace, the answer to their communication difficulties is not far away. The example of Stephen Hawking and the use of technology that has enabled him to continue to communicate is a vital one to remember when working with pupils with very complex learning difficulties. Their difficulties in communication may well be put down to the limitations of the technology.

As mentioned, the cost of keeping pace with technology can be prohibitive, but effective leaders within a number of schools have developed the concept of an e-learning foundation to ensure equality of opportunity with regards to technological access. The implications of this for those working within SEN environments are potentially greater than in mainstream schools as there is often the need for highly individualised and, therefore, high-cost ICT equipment for the pupil. All of this means the establishment of e-learning foundations, or alternative funding streams, to ensure access at home and at school, and this is vital to ensure that this significant aspect of the future special school is established.

ICT has great potential to nurture the development of the individual by encouraging pupils to take responsibility for their learning. Technology provides enjoyable opportunities for many pupils to be more fully involved in a range of learning experiences. It also allows them to chart individual progress against

> **CASE STUDIES**
>
> **Addington School:**
>
> - has laptops for all teachers;
> - has introduced the use of interactive whiteboards; and
> - has an access and ICT Support Teacher who has a coaching role within the school.
>
> **Kingfisher School:**
>
> - has purchased four interactive whiteboards and has trialled these with the use of Espresso, an on-line education package; and
> - uses PowerPoint to develop Talking Books.
>
> **Holyport Manor School:**
>
> - has employed an ICT manager with an industry background and high level of knowledge and expertise – staff are to think of what they want to achieve and the ICT manager will aim to make it happen.

targets they have been involved in setting. The ongoing development of Integrated Learning Systems has great potential benefit for pupils with special needs. Alongside this needs to be heeded the warning that some pupils, particularly those with Autistic Spectrum Disorder, can become obsessed with the use of a computer and can see it as a useful tool to reduce the need for social interaction. When used wisely it can also be a very useful tool in exploring ways of reducing social isolation.

As identified earlier, the further development of ICT will lead to a reduction of barriers to learning and an increase in opportunities for those with SEN to participate more fully through such technological advances as voice-activated software and touch-sensitive screen technologies. This will also be enhanced through the further development of individual set-ups for increased computer access, through switches and rollerballs etc. There will also be increased communication opportunities through the continued development of both hi-tech and low-tech communication aids appropriate to the needs of the individual. The effective leader of the SEN environment will look to bring in staff with the necessary skills as well as encourage others to develop their ICT skills. Whereas at one time many authorities and districts had identified consultants who were able to provide and recommend ICT hardware and software for individual pupils, in the majority of cases this expertise now resides in SEN environments. The forward-looking, effective leaders in these environments have used this expertise to the advantage of the pupils in their own settings as well as in partner settings. They have also used it to raise additional funds which are identified in the case study material.

CASE STUDIES

Crosshills Technology College has a new building which will include:

- work bases with pods for laptops;
- interactive whiteboards in many classes;
- an e-library;
- a huge screen with the ability to video-conference;
- a media studies centre; and
- an on-line centre.

Severndale School has:

- a Communication Aids Project assessment centre; and
- an ICT manager who provides INSET courses.

The development of Managed Learning Environments that enable the provision of personalised feedback and target setting has already become well-established in many mainstream schools. The next phase of this development will ensure that the MLE is appropriate and accessible to all pupils with SEN. Some leaders of SEN environments have already begun to work either in partnership with providers or on their own to develop the structure of an MLE that can truly meet the individual needs of the pupil. The full extent to which these can be used effectively will vary within each SEN setting, and for some, like the Pupil Referral Unit (PRU), it may well prove to be highly beneficial in tracking individual progress and assisting in returning to the mainstream.

There has been a significant increase in the use of presentation technologies, which, when used effectively, can overcome inhibitions and disabilities that might otherwise hinder development. One example of how this can be successfully demonstrated is by developing presentational skills through the use of technologies such as interactive whiteboards. Interactive whiteboards, whilst proving very motivating and beneficial to mainstream pupils, are becoming a vital tool within many SEN environments. The motivational aspect for many pupils of being actively involved in their learning cannot be overestimated, as for many of these pupils the nature of passively receiving the lesson content has inhibited their inclusion in mainstream lessons. For other pupils with complex learning difficulties the ability to see images that have particular relevance to them on a large screen, to negate possible visual difficulties, brings lessons to life. A number of skilled staff within SEN environments have also been using PowerPoint to create talking books that pupils can access through the use of switches.

The use of video-conferencing is being used to significant effect in a small number of special schools. Those SEN environments which cater for pupils who are school refusers or for whom the mainstream system cannot cater are beginning to explore the use of video-conferencing further, and it was suggested by one head teacher that it could be used to help give pupils with Autistic Spectrum Disorder access to mainstream lessons where otherwise, because of their difficulties with social interaction, they would not cope. There are many who are not yet totally convinced about its widespread use with pupils but, given the large geographical distances between many special schools, it has great potential as a means of networking schools and sharing professional training and development opportunities.

The outsourcing of ICT-related services is a possible area of revenue raising which most SEN environments have not yet targeted. Some SEN environments have a set business plan to market their ICT training facilities to local businesses. A number have also employed ICT specialists from outside education and given them a brief to build a successful ICT provision within the school alongside clear targets for raising revenue from external sources. As one commented, 'the only real limitation is our creativeness; if you can think of an idea the technology is now out there to deliver it'.

On-line delivery of teaching resources that reflect the school's strengths and/or specialisms have been developed by a number of schools, and specialist staff have been deployed. In one school, their Access and ICT specialist teacher was available for individual assessments, school professional development and advisory work to other schools and the LEA.

The use of ICT with staff in school is an area in which great strides have been made in a number of SEN environments by leaders with a clear vision of the role and purpose of ICT in their settings. These leaders most often articulate the fact that the greatest strides were made when laptops were made available to all teachers as a minimum requirement, and they were then provided with the necessary technical support. Many schools are also beginning to develop the provision of an intranet, which may be externally provided and maintained, that has all teacher information and materials available for easy access and helps reduce teacher workload. It will have all the schemes of work with linked internet or other relevant resources, available by broadband to ensure speed of access.

Schools are also developing ICT professional development courses which are

CASE STUDY

Blackfriars School:

- shares ICT expertise with the wider community via the school's role as a Ukonline Centre;
- offers ICT assessments for special needs pupils in any school;
- offers to mainstream schools advice on the most appropriate hardware, peripherals and software for SEN pupils;
- offers access to a resource bank for a limited loan period;
- offers to mainstream schools pupil and staff support, for a fixed period of time, in the use of ICT; and
- has a telephone, fax, e-mail and website information service.

available to their staff and other schools and form part of an accredited course. These are available on-line or as taught courses, or a mixture of both.

A number of leaders were also clear that ICT could be seen as a tool or a weapon by staff and themselves. The widely espoused reduction in paperwork going into schools has just been replaced by an increasing amount of e-mails containing more paperwork than the original mailings. It is important for leaders and others to use the right communication method in any situation. Many have been caught out by the hastily composed e-mail which has been sent before appropriate thinking has taken place.

The final area related to ICT is linked to the previous chapter on Partnerships. The development of networks of schools – special with special, and special with mainstream – is already well developed in an increasing number of areas. The concept of developing connected learning communities will further develop the role and purpose of these networks. Effective leaders in SEN environments are encouraging their settings to participate in innovative curriculum initiatives and the development of advantageous partnerships with other schools and institutions at home and abroad. The purpose of these will be to provide on-line information, courses and contacts for pupils and staff to further develop opportunities, knowledge, skills and attitudes.

As can be seen, there are many advantages that can be gained by the effective leader for his/her own setting through the purchase, use and development of hardware, software and skills. There are also inherent dangers that must be heeded, such as the costly mistake made by some in purchasing hardware that is quickly superseded. The advantages that have been shown throughout this chapter far outweigh the risks, particularly for the wise leader who is either informed enough to make judicious decisions or knows someone who is!

Summary

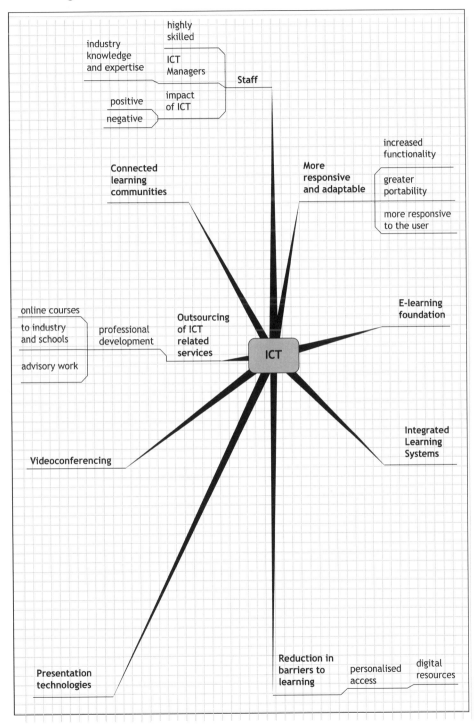

Figure 3.2 ICT summary

Innovation

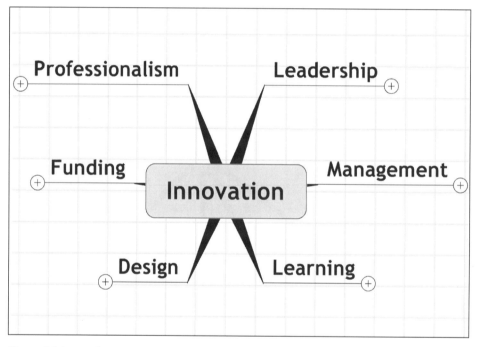

Figure 4.1 Innovation

> The integrating concept is change. Drucker (1999:73) contends that the only ones who
> will survive in a period when change is the norm will be the change leaders, for 'to be a
> successful change leader an enterprise has to have a policy of systematic innovation'.
>
> (Caldwell 2002)

In his paper, Caldwell (2002) identified a number of key areas of innovation that
he felt were going to be vital for the development and growth of schools. In this
chapter a number of these are explored with specific reference to the SEN sector.

There has undoubtedly been a significant shift in the educational world towards encouraging greater creativity and innovation. Many educational leaders have not, so far, grasped this opportunity, probably for one of two reasons: an *inability* to 'think outside of the box'; or a *fear* of 'thinking outside of the box'.

For many leaders and staff within educational settings these factors may well be entwined, as for a number of years now they have been told *what* to teach, *how* to teach it and *when* to teach it. Anyone venturing outside this strict dictum needed to be brave, courageous or foolish, depending on the outcome of doing so. The rhetoric from government is starting to change, but unless the monitoring systems put in place, such as Ofsted, fully reflect this new-found belief in educational leaders to make professionally informed decisions, then it will remain rhetoric. While this may sound negative, it was found that the most successful leaders in a range of SEN environments were very creative and had built a policy of systematic innovation into their settings. A number of the leaders noted that in many ways it was easier for leaders in SEN environments to be innovative, as either the pupils had not responded to inflexible mainstream environments or national initiatives often did not consider the SEN population, and therefore they were justified in picking and choosing what was to be implemented.

What was also clear was that the leadership of the SEN environments needed to foster and encourage risk taking to build innovative settings. One of the ways that successful leaders of SEN fostered this feeling was through the development of strategic intentions. This gave staff a clear long-term vision of where they were headed without being overly restrictive. It was reported that this enabled them to feel empowered to innovate within these boundaries. The leaders of SEN environments were also innovative in their development of strategic leadership at all levels through increasing the awareness and intellectual capacity within the organisation. Through this leadership development their environments were enabled to develop innovative capacity and to respond in a quicker way. The promotion of strategic partnerships has already been covered to a large extent in the chapter on Partnerships and is one innovative approach that successful leaders of SEN environments will need to adopt if they are to flourish and grow.

Many would see the inclusion of management in a chapter on innovation as something of an anomaly, but it has become an underestimated need within all educational environments since the 'rise' of leadership. But leadership was seen to be most successful within the SEN environments that had well-established management systems that were also innovative in their design. One of the key challenges for all schools, in terms of innovation in management, is in the area of 'knowledge management'. The development of successful knowledge management involves the school developing capacity among its entire staff to be at the forefront of knowledge in respect of learning and teaching, and leadership approaches; in fact with regard to all the other areas of innovation described in

CASE STUDIES

Severndale School:

● has fostered strategic partnerships with a number of SEN-focused companies – Smirthwaite, Intergrex, Spacekraft.

Mary Elliot School:

● has explicitly used Futures Thinking to develop a 3–5-year plan identifying five strategic intents with the intention of developing capacity within the school.

Holyport Manor School:

● is developing the idea of staff acting as consultants in:
    ICT
    Social Communication Disorders, including ASD
    Equal Opportunities, including complex challenging behaviour.

this chapter. It is also the systems that are built to share this knowledge that enable the setting to truly develop intellectual capacity. This 'intellectual capacity' is then used to improve performance both within the school and with its partnership establishments. An in-depth understanding of systems was demonstrated by a number of the successful leaders of SEN environments and this was allied to policies and procedures that were:

● Robust
● Shared
● Understood
● Agreed
● Implemented

This ensured that all staff were secure within their environment and able to build capacity as a consequence.

> The illiterate of the year 2000 will not be the individual who cannot read or write, but the one who cannot learn, unlearn and relearn.
>
> (Alvin Toffler, in Prashnig 1998)

This area of learning is central to all educational environments and, by their very nature, SEN settings are well placed to use innovative approaches to assist the learning of the pupils within them. There were a number of innovative approaches that the successful leaders of SEN environments were encouraging

CASE STUDIES

Addington School:

- has a School Improvement Group with two strands in which any member of staff can participate in time-specific projects:
  Teaching and Learning Forum
  Research and Development Forum;
- has a Data Manager – developing the school's Autumn Package for use in assessing value added.

Coxlease School:

- Development of Post-16 provision – staff put some money into the development of this subsidiary and then gain some potential additional financial reward in return for developing high-quality provision.
- Involvement of Principal Steve Cliffen on National Executive of NAES leading to discussions with Charles Clarke on areas such as:
  Regional Partnerships
  recruitment and retention issues in EBD
  working with CAMHS
  curriculum flexibility
  continuum of provision – PRU to Independent.

and developing. In spite of these it was recognised that there was still much to be done in developing further.

Too often education is thought about as what takes place in educational institutions and we forget how much concurrent learning takes place in the home, the workplace and the community. There is a need to discover what prior learning there is on which to build, as well as how to build on it. SEN environments are generally much more effective at doing this, and the links between school, home and respite are already well established.

While this is the case, most leaders of SEN environments would also acknowledge that there needs to be further development to ensure learning activities are integrated between the pupil's different environments. Some environments, with the support of additional funding, were developing home–school liaison posts to ensure that there is a co-ordinated, integrated learning package on offer to the pupils.

Within the current UK educational environment there is much talk about developing an individualised programme for all pupils with:

- schools as gateways to networked provision; and

- schools as 'solutions assemblers' in a personalised system.

If it is to develop further, then all educational environments, and stakeholders, will need to acknowledge the blurring of boundaries as to where learning takes place. With an acknowledgement of learning taking place in a variety of situations through a variety of media, there are a range of new and different opportunities to enhance the learning experiences available to education providers.

The development of partnership provision with its collaborative approach to pupil learning and teaching means that for each pupil's education programme, delivery will need to become more flexible. Therefore, the base school and teacher can be seen to be the physical hub of a learning environment that for some pupils may include a virtual element. As can be seen in the case study material, a number of SEN environments are well ahead of the game in responding to individual needs, and most would accept that a major strength of most SEN environments is their ability to respond to individual needs. What is not always the case is the use of partnership provision to further extend opportunities for all pupils with SEN.

Throughout education there is becoming a greater focus on pupils taking control of their learning. This is more complex, but no less important, in the field of those working with pupils with SEN. Successful SEN environments are exploring ways and means of collecting pupils' views with regards to all school matters, including developing capacity within the pupils to make informed choices and decisions about their learning.

There has been a significant amount of research leading to an increased understanding of learning. This has obvious relevance in all phases of education, but the particular issue for those leading the SEN environment is how to transfer this information to ensure that it has relevance to pupils with special educational needs.

CASE STUDY

Addington School:

- has a Whole-School Co-ordinator whose focus is on Multiple Intelligences and Learning Styles. It achieved the following:

    the introduction of drinking bottles from the research about the brain and the need for water to aid concentration and learning;

    the introduction of a physical exercise regime before the start of each school day;

    delivery of whole-school training to all staff; and

    delivery of an information session to parents on learning styles.

There have been huge increases in our knowledge of the brain and how it normally develops and learns, but the challenge for all within education is to ensure that this is put into daily practice within our educational environments. We would expect our doctor or surgeon to have access to, and understanding of, the most recent knowledge and research and to implement this, but do we expect the same of our teachers in SEN environments? The evidence is that the most successful leaders in SEN settings are attempting to address this shortfall.

The knowledge on multiple intelligences is starting to be used by some SEN environments within the assessment process as it recognises the strengths within each individual. The current deficit model, most often used, states a pupil's needs with little recognition of their strengths. These SEN environments report on the different intelligences and ensure that all stakeholders are kept up to date and informed as to what the different areas are and mean.

There have also been significant increases in the knowledge and understanding of learning styles and their application to a range of educational settings. Many effective teachers of pupils with SEN used a range of learning styles to try and assist the learning of their pupils without fully recognising what they were doing. The current research and expanding knowledge base ensured that their approaches were authenticated and further developed. The area that needs further research and development is in the area of understanding how people learn in natural and authentic situations, as a significant area of difficulty for many pupils with special educational needs is the generalisation of skills.

The successful leaders of SEN environments have also ensured that the developing knowledge and understanding of learning then impacts on the pedagogical approaches used by their staff and is also built into the curriculum.

These leaders had allowed, and positively encouraged, staff to explore how these new innovations were to be implemented into the educational setting in which they worked. In spite of some interesting approaches being developed, there was little evidence seen of the development of a specific 'learn how to learn' course for pupils with SEN. While it is acknowledged that this is no easy task, surely such a course would aid their development. Also, although the use of technology to enhance learning is explored in more detail in the ICT chapter, it is important to note that leaders of SEN environments must ensure that they provide a blended learning experience rather than relying too much, or not enough, on technology.

Successful leaders in SEN environments could see the developments regarding the understanding of learning as a real opportunity to develop a 'curriculum for learning' which recognises the existence of multiple intelligences and establishes learning to learn courses, incorporating the teaching of, and making explicit use of, 'thinking skills'.

Oxfordshire PRUIS Curriculum Framework: a model

We have identified four overlapping cornerstones which, together, form the PRUIS Curriculum and enable us to fulfil our vision and aim. The cornerstones of the PRUIS Curriculum are:

- Behaviour and Personal Development
- Work Related Learning, Citizenship and Life Skills
- Core Academic Curriculum
- Entitlement Curriculum

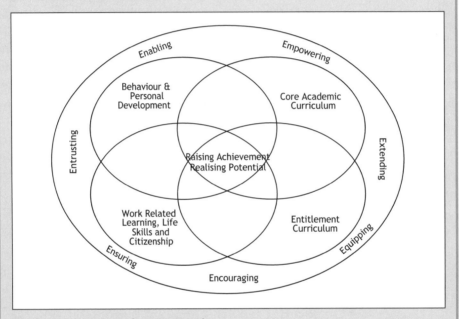

Figure 4.2 PRUIS Curriculum Framework

The above diagram shows how each of the cornerstones overlap. There will be many activities which cut across these boundaries and pupils need access to all elements. However, for each individual pupil there will be different balances of the elements to reflect need, timescale and context.

Through discussion with leaders of SEN environments, and from reading recent literature, the concept of professional learning communities was seen as crucial in not only developing the innovative approaches and knowledge of learning, but also, as importantly, in embedding the practice into the setting. The four strands of a learning organisation, as identified by Brighouse (2000), clearly identify what a professional learning community looks like:

- talk about teaching;
- observe each other teaching;
- plan, organise, deliver and evaluate together; and
- teach each other.

The challenge for the leader of the SEN environment, particularly within small special schools and those working in the SEBD sector, is to make this happen.

It is also true to say that in a learning society all communities have to be learning communities and therefore the effective leader of the SEN environment needs to use their 'boundary spanning' skills to help develop the above strands across all the learning environments with which the pupils engage. Systems, policies and procedures were developed across environments that had strong partnership arrangements to ensure that the experience, knowledge and skills were shared across and between these partnerships. It was noted by more than one leader that the SEN environment must become the centre for the development of learning and teaching knowledge for all pupils, but particularly for those with SEN.

When learning is discussed within education it is too often presumed that it is related only to the pupils. It was made clear from discussions with SEN leaders that there needs to be a paradigm shift to ensure that there is a shared understanding that personal learning takes place for everyone, continuously.

The concept of lifelong learning has been advocated and discussed in many media and there are few who would argue against it. Successful leaders of SEN environments were clear that they needed to model this if they were to expect their staff to be open to continued learning. This was demonstrated in a variety of ways. One leader undertook to do an additional course of further education each time a member of staff did. Another undertook research and ensured this was fed back to staff through an innovative approach to meetings which encouraged all staff to attend and then undertake research themselves, hence building the idea of everyone as a researcher. All the research undertaken was trialled in a number of classrooms with the outcomes becoming incorporated into practice.

Learning, curriculum and pedagogy cannot be seen in isolation and it is in the area of design – how schools are organised – that innovation is highly influential. There must be an acknowledgement of the changes needed in leadership and management, resourcing of schools, links with other establishments and the community. All of these need to be focused on developing informed learning and teaching through an outcomes-orientated curriculum brought to life through ICT. The changing role of teachers and the development of professional learning teams within SEN environments will lead to these settings being seen as the leaders in this innovative design, including the use of teaching assistants as one such example. The professional learning teams will acknowledge and develop the links with an increasing range of professionals and para-professionals – again an area that successful leaders of SEN environments have done much to promote.

CASE STUDIES

Blackfriars School:

- provides day centre opportunities for profoundly disabled young people aged 19–25;
- provides a specialist outreach and support role to physically/medically impaired pupils in mainstream schools;
- has a Service Level Agreement with the authority to provide physical disability outreach support – now the biggest department in the school;
- has franchise arrangements with a local FE provider for the delivery of a post-19 course;
- plans further post-19 developments, including being funded by LSC as an independent specialist status provider and developing provision for Stoke LEA.

Crosshills Technology College:

- has strong links with the local community which have helped bring in significant additional funding (see funding case study, p. 41);
- is developing a Training Centre Model, looking at bringing in outside presenters.

From discussion with leaders of SEN environments, a number of them lamented the difficulties in being able to establish an innovative approach to governance, not felt by those working within the independent sector. The boundary spanning concept of the 'full-service school', identified in Chapter 2, was seen as the most common-sense evolution for those schools dealing with pupils with the most profound and complex needs. The development of a wraparound provision to meet the needs of the individual and their family would be more achievable. While this is currently not possible within the maintained sector, a number of successful leaders had developed innovative approaches to governance in spite of the difficulties. (See case study material for examples of how successful leaders are pushing at the boundaries.)

The necessity to build partnerships has been covered in detail in the appropriately named chapter, but it is worth noting again here that successful leaders of all SEN environments could not speak highly enough of the need to build strategic partnerships for pupils and staff. The development of co-located provision in Oxfordshire has taken place over many years in a number of the special schools, but this has often come down to the relationships between particular head teachers and the desire, usually initiated by the SEN leader, to make things happen for pupils with SEN. The development and changing need of co-location arrangements can be seen through the case study below.

CASE STUDY

Work undertaken by subsequent head teachers of, first, Bennett House School, and, more recently, Kingfisher School in Abingdon:

1981   Co-location set-up in local primary school due to positive relationships between heads – full inclusion with staff and pupils fully integrated within the staffing and class structure – separate space available for additional support requirements. In 1999 this fully integrated model was abandoned as it could no longer meet the needs of pupils with SLD. The pupils with MLD were now on the primary school roll.

1989   Integrated nursery set up at a different primary school.

1997   Key Stage 1 class established in the same primary school due to success of integrated nursery and desire of parents to see their children with SEN remain within a mainstream environment.

1999   Key Stage 2 class established with their own classroom built on the mainstream site.

2004   Key Stage 3 still to be decided due to a range of difficulties in finding a willing and able secondary provision.

A number of other leaders of SEN environments who had been successful in developing partnership arrangements also noted great difficulty in developing co-located or partnership provision for secondary-aged pupils. The author would like to recognise that in his personal experience as head teacher of Addington School, significant success had been achieved in developing partnership provision with a couple of secondary schools within Wokingham District Council. Some of this success was undoubtedly due to the Specialist Schools Initiative, as discussed earlier, but it was also due to a belief on behalf of the two head teachers that stronger links were the right thing for both schools and this was leading to the development of a satellite class on one site for secondary-aged pupils.

There must also be a drive by leaders from all SEN environments to develop networks, both nationally and internationally. Nationally, the formation and development of the National College for School Leadership (NCSL) has undoubtedly assisted in enabling like-minded leaders to interact with each other, including the sharing of links across a range of public sector environments. While this is extremely welcome – along with the possibilities it provides in funding research such as that undertaken by the author – successful leaders across the range of SEN environments all spoke passionately about the need to develop networks to ensure they did not become isolated and/or forgotten. Many held senior positions on national bodies such as the Leading Edge Steering Group, Specialist Schools Steering Group or NCSL Leadership Network, to enable them to fully contribute to discussions and developments on a national scale. A number also ensured that they had partnerships with colleagues from outside the education sector to ensure they did not become blinkered within the SEN and education environments.

CASE STUDIES

Education Leeds

- Leeds is organised into five 'wedges' to encourage co-working between schools and a real mix of schools. Each wedge has a Specialist Inclusive Learning Centre which provides:
    a range of EY, Primary, Secondary and Post-16 Partnerships;
    no child of pre- or post-compulsory aged schooling to be on a segregated site.

Oxfordshire PRUIS

- Six small PRUs became one PRU and Integration Service bringing collective control of destiny and service to schools and enabling a more flexible provision to be established.

Holyport Manor School

- Part of a federation of five secondary schools – staff from Holyport acting as Behaviour Consultants.

Coxlease School:

- is looking at opportunities to become a training provider with the purchase of an Outdoor Education Centre for team building and personal development;
- is developing franchising opportunities.

LEAs and schools buy into the Coxlease School arrangement and have access to policies/structures/systems and consultancy.

Another common thread was that of developing international partnerships. Although it would be over-simplistic to think that one system of education can just be transposed into another environment, there are many valuable lessons that can be learned from looking at innovative practice worldwide, and the establishment of global learning networks is vital in enabling this to happen. One such example is that of the International Networking for Educational Transformation (iNet) which has recently been established by the Specialist Schools Trust and covers a number of schools across a range of countries including England, Australia and Singapore.

CASE STUDIES

Perth, Western Australia:

- is building new inclusive campuses co-located with mainstream schools, where possible. The current range of provision is as follows: an Education Support School (own site and Principal), an Education Support Centre (co-located with own Principal) and an Education Support Unit (co-located with Team Leader).

Ballajura Community College, Perth, Australia

- The Inclusive Learning Team is a whole-school team within Ballajura Community College and is a new innovation in the education of students with disabilities. It consists of a team leader, four education support teachers, 11 education assistants and two social trainers.

Port Phillip Specialist School, Melbourne, Australia:

- has implemented the 'fully serviced school' concept with a Head of Integrated Service, a professor with expertise in all aspects of paramedical service delivery and staff with extensive experience in the use of ICT to optimise outcomes for pupils with special needs. The Integrated Service model acknowledges the importance of classroom-based services and allows more students to receive services than by using the traditional models of withdrawal and 1:1 delivery. There is an art centre with a 0.6 art therapist and a dental clinic on-site, and the school has also developed after-school care provision.

The current need to look for innovative and alternative methods of funding our schools, rather than just relying on taxation and public spending, is reliant on longer-term national perspectives on how this might be achieved for all schools. There are highly likely to be particular issues around the funding of specialist provision. It would be welcomed by many working within the SEN field if funding was to be multi-agency funding through a more formal agreement of how those agencies are going to meet the needs of the clients within a certain defined geographical area. The need for consistency in relation to the organisation of education, health and social services is probably a prerequisite to this being successfully achieved, and the current initiatives in developing Children's Trusts and the Green Paper *Every Child Matters* (DfES 2003a) are welcomed by most as moving to a more 'joined-up approach' which was advocated by the Labour Government a number of years ago. Unfortunately, from discussion with leaders from a range of different districts and authorities, there still remains a long way to go. Currently there can often be different legal responsibilities and boundaries and subsequent responsibilities for education and health services in particular.

Current innovative approaches to securing additional funding can be found in government strategies such as Specialist School status and the Networked Learning Communities initiative, delivered by NCSL. Additional approaches that special schools have used are to link into community use to fund sports and/or ICT facilities. The use of outsourcing knowledge, skills and experience has been used very creatively by a number of the leaders of SEN environments. It was noted by all that there was a need to carefully balance the outsourcing/outreach development alongside developing capacity within their environments to ensure that the pupils benefited from any such activities. Many of the leaders also noted the need to sometimes 'create demand' by providing a service for a period of time, demonstrate the quality of that service and then, at a later date, require schools and/or authorities to purchase the service in order for it to continue. As in all areas of innovation they recognised the element of risk and that it was often quite high in the early stages, but once quality had been proven the need to self-fund future services for a period of time was reduced.

The teaching profession needs to innovate with regards to the development and implementation of research. There needs to be a move to teachers' work being fully informed by the most recent research. Also, the link between research and practice needs to be strengthened with, as mentioned earlier in this chapter, all staff being seen as researchers, and with lifelong professional learning being seen as the norm. The area of innovation that is being highlighted in this section is that of professionalism. Leaders within all settings need to encourage and develop the notion of research-based practice and also to facilitate opportunities for mainstream colleagues to either undertake work with, or benefit from the experiences and/or knowledge gained from working with, pupils with special needs.

CASE STUDIES

Blackfriars School

- £200k gained from lottery funding to build a sports hall that is open on a Saturday for families.
- New Opportunities Fund (NOF) grant has been acquired to pay for sports hall staff.
- £70k per year is raised through the use of the school as a community resource.
- An ICT Support Manager, who acts as technician/network developer/ trainer/website manager, earns income for the school through his support of mainstream schools.
- The UK Online Centre – open from 4 pm to 8 pm on Thursday – earns income.
- The pool opens from 5 pm to 7.30 pm, five nights a week, for family swimming.
- A day centre for 19–25-year-olds is funded from Social Services and private funds.
- Bid for Technology College status has been made.
- Basic and bespoke training packages delivered for a range of industries which brings in additional funding.
- Leading Edge status achieved.

Crosshills Technology College

- Technology College Status – joint bid.
- £1$\frac{1}{4}$ million build – funded by DfES through identifying community links and development opportunities.
- Funding gained through NOF for a cyber café and a family learning project.
- ICT training packages being delivered for mainstream staff – additional funding gained for this.
- Hiring out of conference facilities to LEA/Social Services/Health has brought in additional £27K.

Severndale School

- The ICT Manager generates income through courses for mainstream colleagues.

CASE STUDIES

Blackfriars School:

● provides professional development support for teachers and teaching assistants to enable mainstream schools to increase their capacity to support inclusion;

● aims to research and share best practice in inclusion through a range of projects.

Severndale School:

● has become a teacher training base, setting up management modules in partnership with HE in response to a recognised need to develop middle and senior managers.

Crosshills Technology College

● Teaching assistants (TAs) are being trained to become lecturers in the new building and unqualified teachers. Three TAs have trained to become counsellors.

Addington School:

● has become an Accredited NVQ Training and Assessment Centre:
    to develop own staff competencies and also as a centre for mainstream training; and
    to provide support and advice to other LEAs and schools who are looking at setting up their own centres.

Ballajura Community College:

● has established an Inclusive Learning Team to meet the needs of all pupils within its community.

The research on multiple intelligences as it relates to innovation in learning was discussed earlier in this chapter. This also has direct consequences for how leaders view the staff, and their knowledge, skills and experiences, to ensure all intelligences are recognised within their SEN environments. The concept of multiple intelligences has also been ascribed to schools, and leaders wishing to develop these capacities within their environments would be well advised to further explore the concept of the intelligent school, as described in the paper by Caldwell (2002), with its multiple intelligences of:

● contextual
● strategic

- academic
- reflective
- pedagogical
- collegial
- emotional
- spiritual
- ethical

The final aspect that is worth consideration, particularly for those working within the field of SEN, is the making of decisions and the taking of actions that are data-driven. Those working within mainstream education, and some SEN settings, have become well-used to the use of data to explore approaches and interventions, and their success or lack of it. This has been a particular challenge for those working with pupils who are 'working towards Level 1' of the National Curriculum assessment tests and tasks. It was yet another example of pupils with SEN not being thought about at the launch of a national initiative.

Thankfully, despite their many critics and shortcomings, the introduction of P-levels enabled some meaningful data to be collected by special schools. The use of these data is still in its infancy in many SEN environments but there are some examples of innovative approaches to the collection and use of the data. For many, the challenge remains to ensure that the data used are meaningful in terms of number of pupils and that it is used thoughtfully and wisely and does not detract from that which SEN environments do best – meeting individual needs. It was clear from a number of the leaders that the need to develop robust data was an imperative if informed decisions and comparisons were to be made, with the key purpose being to identify, develop and share best practice in meeting the needs of pupils with SEN.

Summary

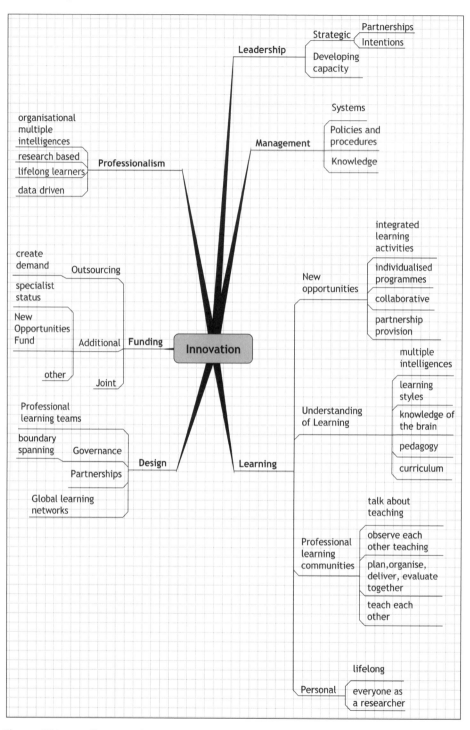

Figure 4.3 Innovation summary

The additional leadership challenges of different settings

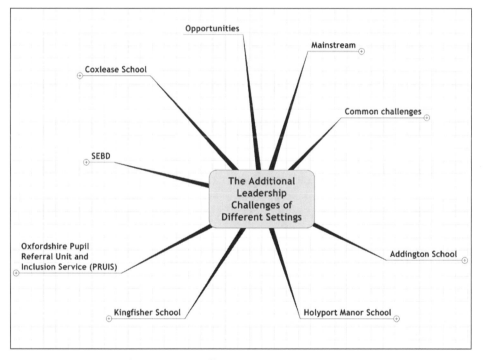

Figure 5.1 The Additional Leadership Challenges of Different Settings

The field of special education faces deep changes in relation to its thinking and practices.
(Mel Ainscow in 'Developing inclusive schools: implications for leadership' – NCSL essay, May 2000)

At the outset of this chapter it must be recognised that the additional leadership challenges that will be outlined are drawn from the views of a small, but select, group of successful SEN leaders. It is clear to anyone who has worked in a number of different SEN settings that context is everything and that there can be as much that is different between supposedly similar settings as there is in common. This chapter attempts to explore the areas identified as additional challenges in the different settings alongside a brief outline of the setting the leader is talking about. What may also be seen is that there are a significant number of common challenges for those working within SEN settings, particularly those in special schools and PRUs. In line with the attitude of successful leaders of SEN environments each section finishes with opportunities identified. This, alongside the chapter on 'SEN provision in the future', explores possible solutions to the challenges faced.

The first area we will consider is that of the mainstream setting. The contextual background of the mainstream setting, as well as the differences between primary and secondary, can vary so much that this is only an attempt to draw some common challenges faced by leaders of SEN in these environments. It is also important to identify what is meant by leaders of SEN in mainstream settings; it is often the person whose job title is Special Educational Needs Co-ordinator, or SENCO to give the post its usual title. What is also clear from discussions with mainstream head teachers and from reading current literature is that rarely, if ever, can the SENCO make a significant difference without the overt support of the head teacher or at least the deputy head.

For the primary school this should be less of a problem as the head or deputy head is usually the SENCO as well, although larger primary schools may well have a separate SENCO. Evidence suggests that although the head may be the SENCO as well, and therefore status is not an issue, it is how they act in their role as SENCO, the resources targeted towards SEN and the climate they build that identify whether this is a positive outcome or a challenge.

For the larger primary school, and virtually all secondary schools, the status assigned to the role of SENCO is often a major challenge to developing SEN provision within the school. In a few enlightened schools the SENCO sits on the leadership team and therefore has a direct input into decision-making and a chance to make an impact. Through this role they have, with the support of the head teacher, the chance to build the climate of the school. Therefore the role of the head teacher is crucial in the building of an inclusive school climate.

There are often more significant SEN leadership issues within the secondary environment due to the structure of these schools and the inflexibilities inherent within them. It has also been clear from discussions with mainstream colleagues that the need to create opportunities to develop SEN provision within secondary schools can be developed with the right attitude and approach from senior staff.

The area of stakeholder expectations can also be an additional challenge to those leading SEN within the mainstream environment. This is multi-faceted and the different stakeholders can have opposing views. Parents can often be concerned about the rise in numbers of pupils with SEN or the pupil with SEN already within the school who is particularly challenging the environment at that moment. These concerns can range from the unfounded belief that too many 'kids with special needs' will impact on educational attainment, to the much more understandable concern about the pupil who may be physically attacking other pupils. It takes a strong leader, with clearly articulated and demonstrated beliefs, to win over parents and governors.

It has often been commented that the most significant barrier to promoting inclusion is that of league tables and target setting, and it is perhaps the most significant additional challenge faced by leaders of SEN in mainstream environments. In a perverse sort of way it was found, from the research undertaken by the author, that the most inclusive mainstream schools were often to be found within the most challenging inner-city schools where the student population was so diverse that the inclusion of pupils with SEN was seen as a matter of course, whereas within highly academic authorities the pressure to not only maintain but also to further improve targets led to the inclusion of pupils with SEN being seen as more of a problem. There was a particularly interesting juxtaposition between the LEA 'encouraging' schools to achieve better national target results while at the same time discouraging schools from excluding pupils with SEN. For many, these were understandably seen as competing priorities.

Those mainstream leaders who were committed to promoting inclusion usually did so for a number of reasons: they had an uncompromising commitment and belief in inclusive education; and the differences among students and staff were perceived as a resource. The author, from personal experience, also noted that direct collaboration and partnership with an SEN environment was often undertaken to build capacity in meeting the needs of the pupils with SEN within the mainstream environments. One secondary school leader explored the idea of satellite classes on his site along with possible discussions on the 'franchising' of support for pupils with SEN to the special school.

From discussions with successful leaders of SEN environments, there were a significant number of common challenges faced that were additional to those faced by the majority of mainstream leaders. It has been said that for a head teacher to be successful he/she has to be effective at 'managing the boundaries' and this is particularly true for those working within SEN environments. For most SEN settings there are a significant number of other professionals in addition to teachers, classroom support staff and administrative staff. These can include any or all of the following:

● speech and language therapists
● physiotherapists
● occupational therapists

- teachers for the visually impaired
- teachers for the hearing impaired
- school nurse
- counsellors
- therapists

While there is often not enough of the relevant therapists to meet the needs of the pupils within the SEN environment, it must also be recognised that they can often come from a different cultural background and have their own agenda. Therefore an ability to manage the different cultures and multiple agendas is a prerequisite for a successful leader of SEN. Put this alongside the fact that with the above-named professionals it is often the case – apart from the independent sector – that they are managing people whom they do not employ. This can be a particular challenge when building a community from such a disparate group of people, a challenge successfully met by a number of leaders of SEN environments.

SEN settings also tend to have a great deal of visitors, much more than the mainstream setting, and while many of the leaders welcomed this as a way of reducing the barriers it was also recognised that it needed to be watched carefully. This was particularly the case when encouraging inter-agency working with Social Services and/or Health Services. While this was positively encouraged, it was also carefully managed to ensure that the demands placed on the teachers' time were not too great and therefore were not impacting on their teaching role.

The demands of parents can be wide and varied in all educational settings but it was noted that there were particular challenges faced by those leading in SEN environments. All those interviewed were keen to stress the level of empathy needed to have an understanding of the immense pressures faced by the parents of a child with SEN. Many of the parents had to fight the system to get the support they required for their child and this, understandably, ensured that they were often very clear and succinct about what their child needed. It was also recognised that the expectations of parents from many mainstream settings could often not be replicated in terms of offering voluntary support in classrooms, Parent–Teacher Associations and such like, as the time their child was at school was a period of 'respite' for many. There were also the additional complications of finding childcare that enabled the parent to attend evening functions. It was also noted that for many parents, often those whose children had either Social, Emotional and Behavioural Difficulties (SEBD) or Moderate Learning Difficulties (MLD), or a combination of these, school had been a negative personal experience, and the thought of coming back into a school to see a teacher, let alone the head teacher, could be very intimidating. Effective leaders of SEN environments had explored ways of reducing these pressures or at least building understanding among their staff.

The challenge of change has been covered in great detail earlier in this book, but while this is a challenge for all leaders in education there are particular additional challenges that leaders of SEN environments face. There does appear to be more change within the SEN environment, including the requirement to be able to 'manage the unknown'. There are certain issues that arise for leaders of SEN environments that are highly unlikely to be faced by the mainstream leader, including those covered earlier in this chapter, as well as a lack of clarity regarding the role of special schools. A number of successful leaders noted the fact that although they could be recognised as 'excellent' by Ofsted, and be a Leading Edge School, they could still face closure if a review of SEN provision took place within their authority or district and a shift in policy followed.

There was also a perceived lack of support and/or challenge identified by a number of leaders. The lack of support was often due to a lack of knowledge and expertise within the LEA, for maintained schools, and this in turn meant that there was no-one able to challenge the SEN environment appropriately. There was often not a clear vision as to the role of the SEN environments within the LEA and many leaders noted the fact that they were creating an SEN vision for the LEA; but whether this was financially supported was highly debatable. The role of Ofsted was talked about by all the leaders interviewed, not unsurprisingly considering the impact it can, and often does, have. For many years Ofsted was high on challenge but support was virtually non-existent, and there remain concerns about the depth of knowledge and experience of some inspectors given the immensely diverse nature of SEN environments. In the early years a high proportion of SEN environments were deemed to be failing or have serious weaknesses. Fortunately, the number of these has significantly dropped, and this is in part due to leaders becoming more astute as to what is required, alongside a 'reinventing' of Ofsted to encompass more school self-evaluation and improving inspectors' knowledge.

A remaining additional Ofsted challenge for those working within SEN environments, and one that is highly likely to remain, is the fact that what most head teachers see as the major reason for their schools' existence is squeezed into three brief sub-sections of the inspection reports (Cole *et al.* 1998):

● Spiritual, moral, social and cultural development is a sub-section of 'Quality of Education';

● Attitudes, behaviour and personal development is a sub-section of 'Educational Standards';

● Support, guidance and pupils' welfare is also a sub-section of 'Quality of Education'.

A changing pupil profile was also identified as being a common additional challenge for SEN environments. It is one that is probably true of all educational environments but more so for those in the SEN sector. With the inclusion agenda most mainstream schools are having to cope with pupils with more complex SEN than many have had to face previously, and consequently – apart from those working within the 'high-end need' independent sector – many SEN environments are also having to cope with pupils with increasingly complex SEN. The factors for this are many and varied but include, as always, a close eye being kept on finances alongside the understandable desire to keep pupils within their local community, and thereby more complex pupils in local provision, mainstream and special.

There have also been significant medical advances made and many children who would not have survived previously are now doing so, and educational provision has to adapt to meet their needs. Also, many authorities have reorganised their SEN provision and the general move is towards SEN environments that are able to meet the needs of a wide range of pupils rather than a specific group. While this does provide economies of scale and a gradual shift to a more inclusive system, many staff suddenly find themselves teaching a cohort of pupils whom they are not experienced enough to teach. This has required leaders to re-evaluate the structures they currently have in place to ensure they are appropriate, and the most successful leaders recognise the need for flexible structures that can adapt and change. There is also a significant need for staff re-training to give them the skill they require to meet pupils' needs.

The other key area around staff training identified by many of the leaders of SEN environments was the significantly increased need for additional and ongoing training that mainstream schools do not have to fund or find the time to perform. These were often required to meet Health & Safety regulations, such as Manual Handling, and behaviour management courses that included a physical intervention approach such as Team Teach. These were of a high quality and vital to keeping the environments safe and healthy for pupils and staff, but they were also, understandably, quite costly, and staff were then required to be updated regularly to ensure they did not forget strategies and approaches, and to be informed of improved techniques.

Many leaders also noted the fact that they needed very comprehensive induction and ongoing professional development, as many came from mainstream backgrounds, and although they were good teachers they needed to develop their knowledge of the SEN factor and teaching methods and approaches used within the settings. Those who had involvement in initial teacher training (ITT) were also highly critical about the lack of training offered to newly qualified teachers (NQTs) even in some of the basics of good classroom management, let alone training to become a teacher of pupils with SEN. What was noted as being even more disappointing was the fact that although most ITT courses had SEN modules, these were often not compulsory, and it was often asked how a more inclusive education system was to be established without equipping NQTs with some basic SEN knowledge and skills.

Another major staffing issue identified as a common challenge was that of the lack of staff wishing to undertake leadership opportunities. There was no common understanding as to why this was the case, other than that it was an ageing population in many settings.

The final area of challenge, although not identified by all, is that those working within all SEN environments are more likely to come into contact with child abuse than those working in mainstream environments. Many of the pupils within SEN environments are more vulnerable because of a range of factors including the stresses and challenges they bring to those who come into contact with them, and also, in some cases, their inability to communicate effectively. It is also more likely that leaders working with pupils with Social, Emotional and Behavioural Difficulties (SEBD) will face allegations of abuse, either personally or about their staff. These factors, along with a host of additional factors, place great responsibility on the systems, policies and procedures being effectively put into place by local child protection agencies and those with responsibility within the SEN environments.

CASE STUDY

Addington School

This is a mixed-community special school catering for pupils with moderate, severe, and profound and multiple learning difficulties, aged from 2 to 19 years. The proportion of pupils with more complex needs, such as autism and profound and multiple learning difficulties, has increased by more than 50 per cent in the last five years, with over a third having an autistic spectrum disorder diagnosis. All pupils have a Statement of Special Educational Needs and there are 204 pupils on roll.

The following additional challenges are identified by the author from his time as Head teacher of Addington School. First, there are the challenges of providing education throughout five key stages and having enough knowledge of all of these to ensure that staff, parents and other stakeholders have confidence that decisions taken are based on a secure knowledge base. Key to meeting this challenge is building the right structure to support the five key stages, getting the right people in place and then having confidence in them. The second area is that of Ofsted. While a lot has been covered within this chapter already, the additional element is providing the evidence that the school is able to differentiate successfully to meet the needs of pupils with such diverse special educational needs alongside meeting the different curriculum demands across the five key stages. Again, key to achieving this is getting the right system in place, alongside the need to place ongoing professional development at the core of the school.

The need to bring in additional funding to support partnership developments with mainstream schools, including providing outreach and increasing inclusion opportunities for pupils, was also an additional challenge. The need to bring in additional funding to allow leaders to achieve some of the key aims of their environments was noted by leaders from other maintained special school settings. Examples of how this was achieved are contained within the case study material in the chapters on Partnership and Innovation.

CASE STUDY

Holyport Manor Special School

Holyport Manor School is an all-age generic special school. It has a weekly residential facility that is fully incorporated into the life of the school. The school was reorganised and restructured several years ago in order to embrace aspects of inclusive provision. It now educates all pupils alongside each other in age-appropriate groups, irrespective of levels of need. The school is part of the Maidenhead Federation of Schools alongside the five secondary schools in the town.

Through the Federation, staff from Holyport Manor are involved in supporting colleagues in these schools through coaching and mentoring strategies around aspects of behaviour management and curriculum access. The school has a conference facility which is widely used by colleagues from the LEA and local schools. There is a developing resource base at the school to which schools across the Authority subscribe for curriculum support and access to a wide range of information and materials.

The main additional challenges identified by Head teacher Paul Donkersloot not surprisingly revolved around the residential provision of Holyport Manor. He identified that he was initially a little naïve about the additional challenges that would face him in running a residential school, but this soon changed.

He outlined the fundamental need for these pupils to feel safe and stated that he checked this on a regular basis. He also outlined the challenge in providing a 'home' for the pupils and ensuring the provision was not just an extended school for them. He also noted the very real dangers of being a leader in an environment where there is such a captive, vulnerable audience. This is an area where residential provision has an acknowledged increased risk both in terms of actual abuse taking place and alleged abuse. The introduction of the Care Standards Framework, while creating much additional work, was welcomed by both leaders of residential provision as a good thing in developing higher-quality residential provision based on effective systems, policies and procedures.

The final additional challenge identified by Paul Donkersloot was that of the emotional impact on leaders in residential SEN environments. It is clear to anyone who has spent any time working and leading within an SEN setting that the emotional stresses can be great, and for those working within residential settings they can be even more significant.

Paul, in common with the author, identified that there were significant advantages as well as challenges in being a large, all-age special school. One of these is the economies of scale that they bring about. It is the author's experience, after having worked in a small and a large special school, that possibilities with regards to staffing, such as bringing in specialist teachers of PE and Music, or support teachers in ICT, Behaviour and ASD, are more achievable in the larger setting.

CASE STUDY

Kingfisher School, Abingdon

Kingfisher School is based in Abingdon, Oxfordshire, and provides for pupils aged 2–16, all of whom have a wide range of learning difficulties. The school moved to its new premises in 2002 and has excellent facilities for all of its pupils. Fifty per cent of nursery- and primary-aged pupils are based in a mainstream school and have integration opportunities that are supported by Kingfisher staff. The school has recently successfully retained its Investors in People status.

Ann O'Meara, Head teacher of Kingfisher School, identified a number of additional challenges she faced as the leader of a special school with co-located provision. First, she identified the difficulty of managing multiple sites. There can often be a clash of different cultures between the mainstream school and the special school staff working on the same site, and even if this is not a challenge, the co-ordination of meeting schedules, curriculum responsibilities and other day-to-day issues requires a positive approach by the leader. The support required for special school staff on the mainstream site to ensure that they do not feel disconnected from both the special school main site and the mainstream school should not be underestimated, and Ann was clear about the need to find the right person to thrive in the co-located setting.

The joint appointment of staff to the co-located special provision was a successful approach that had been adopted by Kingfisher School with its co-location partners. It was also crucial to put in place funding arrangements at the very outset of any arrangements. Who is responsible for funding what, and how this is going to be agreed, may seem minor issues when starting a significant new venture such as co-location, but if these areas are not given enough time then they can soon lead to additional problems. Ann also identified that there was a need to manage the expectation in the base special school site, as often there was a misconception that things were better in the co-location setting.

Ann was clear that the relationship with the co-located site head teachers was the key for a successful outcome to be achieved. The establishment of the co-location and agreeing the funding arrangements was only the start and it needed a positive approach by both heads to ensure continued success. Ann also recognised the need to continually ensure that the provision remains appropriate, and sometimes a change of site may be needed if the current provision cannot, for a range of reasons, be flexible enough. More detail on the development of co-location at Kingfisher School is to be found in the chapter on Partnerships.

Finally, Ann went on to state that the constructive relationship with the partnership heads usually ensured that a solution to challenges was found. She also stated that she felt that the additional challenges were well worthwhile as the co-located provision enabled a more appropriate approach for some pupils with SEN to be delivered.

CASE STUDY

Oxfordshire PRUIS

The Oxfordshire PRU and Integration Service provides support to excluded pupils and pupils at risk of exclusion across the county. Working from bases in Abingdon, Banbury and Oxford, it offers pupils a variety of provision from long-term placement in Key Stage 4; to short-term, off-site assessment programmes; to school-based outreach support.

The first major additional challenge identified by Andrew Creese, Head of PRUIS, was that of pulling together a geographically spread and diverse range of provision which had recently come together as PRUIS. This he saw as a five-year programme to build the systems, structures, policies and procedures and to build a cohesive approach to delivery. This was a localised additional challenge, but nevertheless one that was being faced by a number of leaders in PRUs. Andrew was clear that he felt that this new structure and approach would bring tangible results.

Andrew also identified the fact that PRUs do not have the legal status of a school, and while this brings the necessary flexibilities to meet the complex, diverse and ever-changing pupil populations, it also brings a number of additional challenges. PRUs are deemed to be part of an LEA's support services and therefore the relationship between the head and the LEA is crucial. With regards to Ofsted, PRUs have the dubious 'pleasure' of being inspected in their own right as well as during the LEA's inspection. Andrew clearly identified the need for leaders within PRUs to build support networks and advocated the use of the BECTa forum set up for such leaders. More details are available on the PRU website (www.prus.org.uk).

Andrew was clear that PRUs and inclusion services were at their most effective when they were proactive, but his experience and that of other leaders in PRUs was that there was significant reactive expectation from the LEA and colleague head teachers to respond to their immediate problems. He also identified the additional challenge of often having to promote teacher expectations with regard to planning and assessment, as many had come through the era when keeping the pupils occupied and off the streets was good enough. The development of a comprehensive curriculum document, covered in more detail in a case study in the chapter on Innovation, has helped to raise these expectations along with a more flexible approach to recognising pupil achievement.

The final area identified by Andrew was the real difficulties in finding any partnership options with any mainstream settings. This is in common with the experiences of Steve Cliffen, Principal of Coxlease School. The common factor between the two settings is that all the pupils within these environments are identified as having Social, Emotional and Behavioural Difficulties (SEBD).

Before looking at the additional challenges identified by Steve it is worth spending some time looking at the common challenges faced by leaders of SEN environments that cater for pupils with SEBD, as although the provision available to these pupils is necessarily as wide as the continuum of their needs, there are a number of commonalities.

This section draws on the writings of Cliffen (2002) and also Cole *et al.* (1998) and from discussions with a range of head teachers and principals of SEBD provision over a number of years.

(Virtually a whole book could be written on a definition of SEBD, and therefore if you would like more information I would recommend that you look at the two references above as well as those contained within the Further Reading section.) Cliffen identifies that many pupils with SEBD may well be experiencing parallel difficulties with their families and communities as well as their school life and this brings particular additional challenges to those working with them. It has also been noted that the ability of the SEBD setting often spans the same ability range as that of a mainstream school and therefore the challenge of providing an interesting, exciting and challenging (though this element needs to be carefully managed) curriculum is significant. The pupils, by definition, often have significant emotional needs that need to be met, alongside (and sometimes before) their educational needs. The significant additional behavioural challenges faced by those working in SEBD environments should not be underestimated and Amos (in Cole *et al.* 1998) identified the need to have 'rubber boundaries'.

There are also a number of additional staffing challenges that must be recognised. Undoubtedly, the need for a strong leadership team is seen as very important within all educational settings but this is even more important in the SEBD setting. It has been noted by many leaders that the need for a strong deputy head and, in the case of residential provision, head of care is crucial if progress is to be made. Those who found either or both of these positions difficult to fill – another particularly significant issue within the SEBD sector – found improvements much more difficult to be made, with an even greater load falling on the head teacher. As has been mentioned previously, there is the need for the successful leader of the

SEN environment to be effective at managing the boundaries; again, without the strong leadership team there are difficulties in addressing in-school and out-of-school needs.

Recruitment and retention are issues across a range of educational provisions but, again, the impact is more acute in the field of SEBD, and many leaders articulated these as significant issues. Increased recognition through payment was made where possible; a commitment to staff welfare through strong social networks (to enable staff to 'let off steam') and more formal approaches through staff welfare programmes such as the Well-Being Project were all offered. Releasing staff to attend professional development opportunities was also an additional challenge as pupils with SEBD did not cope well with having supply staff.

CASE STUDY

Coxlease School

As part of a national continuum of provision Coxlease School strives to protect and educate boys with emotional, behavioural, social and associated intellectual difficulties. It provides care, education, therapy, welfare, support and related services of the highest standard. Coxlease establishes strong links, collaborative working and co-operation with both placing authorities and parent-carers. Its main objective is to facilitate full inclusion into society and prepare its pupils for integration into the wider community as contributing adults.

Steve Cliffen, Principal of Coxlease School, identified a number of additional challenges he believed were faced by leaders in Independent Residential SEN establishments. Many of the challenges are contained within the previous section on SEBD, but as Coxlease was the 'end of the educational line' for the pupils who attended, many of these challenges are magnified.

Steve identified that there was the additional challenge of financial risk for those principals who were also proprietors, alongside the danger of becoming isolated and out of touch with what was happening within the rest of the educational world. He also articulated that there was the total 'buck stops here' element to the independent residential school principal and proprietor role. He further stated that he did experience some negative feelings from others, as Coxlease was independent, but he was clear that the independent sector occupied a niche within a continuum of need and that it should not be seen as competing with maintained special school provision.

As was identified by Paul Donkersloot, the maintained residential special school head teacher, there are many significant additional challenges faced in running a residential provision. As Coxlease is a 52-week provision, Steve identified the challenge of ensuring that you had the right people in the right place and that they were clear about what was acceptable and what was not.

In common with the other leaders of SEN environments interviewed as a precursor to writing this book, Steve was keen to share solutions to the additional challenges and was even keener to share the opportunities he felt were available from working within his environment.

Steve, as the Principal of a very successful Independent Special School, was clear that he was able to buy into the most relevant training, and also bought in support from the most appropriate individuals. He was also looking at Coxlease becoming a training provider and at purchasing an Outdoor Education Centre to be used with pupils and for team building and personal development for adults. Coxlease had recently established a post-16 provision and staff had been given the opportunity to put some of their own money into it in order to gain possible additional rewards from the subsidiary. He was also exploring the idea of franchising, with schools or authorities able to buy into a Coxlease School arrangement to support them in terms of policies, structures, systems and consultancy.

A positive can-do approach was a common thread to be found among all the successful leaders of SEN environments interviewed. They did not want to focus on problems but rather on solutions, and saw opportunities rather than challenges as the only viable approach. Case study material spread throughout the book gives testament to the success of these leaders in a range of SEN environments.

Summary

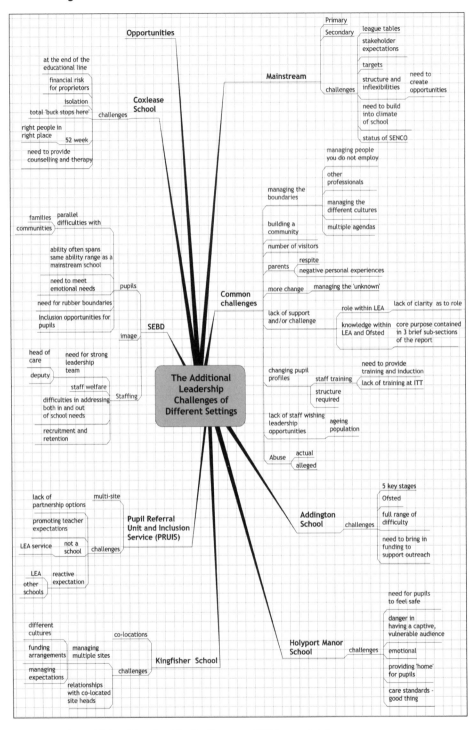

Figure 5.2 The Additional Leadership Challenges of Different Settings summary

Current initiatives and possible impact

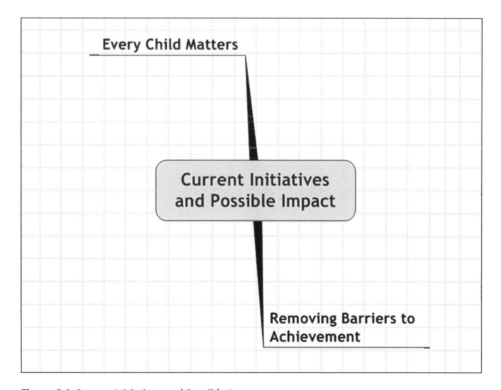

Figure 6.1 Current Initiatives and Possible Impact

This chapter will summarise recent significant initiatives in the UK and then explore, from discussions with leading educators from a range of SEN environments, the possible implications of these. It must be stated here that this chapter is only a brief summary of the different initiatives, and for readers wishing to know more detail they need to refer to the particular documents identified in the Further Reading section.

In the UK, one of the most significant initiatives for all those working with children, but perhaps particularly for those working within SEN environments, is that of *Every Child Matters* (DfES 2003a). In his foreword, the Prime Minister, Tony Blair, identifies that *Every Child Matters* proposes a range of measures to reform and improve children's care, requiring local authorities to bring together, in one place under one person, services for children.

The driving force for the development of *Every Child Matters* was the terrible tragedy of Victoria Climbié and the subsequent Laming Enquiry. While the focus was on developing more effective and efficient child protection policies and procedures, it was clearly identified that this could not be separated from policies to improve children's lives as a whole. The policies arising from the Green Paper are designed to protect children and maximise their potential. What now follows is a brief overview of the main sections with those areas of particular relevance to leaders in SEN environments covered in more detail, with the possible implications identified.

It is worth noting the key outcomes identified by the government after consultation with children and young people. They are as follows:

- being healthy;
- staying safe;
- enjoying and achieving;
- making a positive contribution; and
- economic wellbeing.

The document also identifies a number of actions it is currently taking in order to achieve these outcomes, and some of these deserve further exploration, namely:

- promoting full-service extended schools;
- increasing investment in child and adolescent mental health services (CAMHS); and
- improving speech and language therapy.

As has been discussed in Chapter 2, the idea of the full-service extended schools makes a lot of sense and it is interesting to note the use of 'full service' within this document and the fact that this has developed into the Extended Schools initiative. Whilst the removing of a couple of words may not seem to be particularly important the impact may well be that the UK ends up with a watered-down version of what full-service schools were originally designed to be, an holistic setting meeting the educational, health and social care needs of the family and child. It is worth noting again that SEN environments, whilst being well placed to take on this role, are seemingly often being overlooked in preference to mainstream schools.

The increasing investment in CAMHS is welcomed by leaders within all SEN environments as the stories of lack of support for these children are far too many in number. There remain concerns that this additional support will be targeted at those with 'just' mental health needs, and those with an SEN, as well as a mental health need, will remain short of support.

Leaders were intrigued that speech and language therapy was identified in isolation as opposed to including physiotherapy and occupational therapy, as the experiences recounted identified a need in all three therapies. It was mooted that there were a number of particularly vocal national organisations that had managed to push forward this agenda rather than the therapy agenda *per se*.

The areas of action identified in the Green Paper proposals are as follows:

- supporting parents and carers;
- early intervention and effective protection;
- accountability and integration – locally, regionally and nationally; and
- workforce reform.

Supporting parents and carers

The *Every Child Matters* document identified the government's proposal to consult on a long-term vision to improve parenting and family support through:

- universal services;
- targeted and specialist support; and
- compulsory action.

The area of universal services is focused on schools, health and social care professionals providing information and advice and working with parents to support their child's development. The targeted and specialist support is focused on those parents who have children requiring additional support. The final area of compulsory action is the use of legal means such as Parenting Orders where parents are condoning a child's truancy, anti-social behaviour or offending.

Possible implications

For the leaders interviewed as background to the writing of this book, the provision of the school as a service with the idea of targeted and specialist support is one that is deeply embedded within their environments. The implication is that the support provided to parents will possibly continue to increase, particularly with those that even the successful schools have difficulty engaging with.

As has been discussed earlier, the reasons these particular parents have for not engaging are often quite understandable, and the key is to know when it is necessary to explore additional ways and when these parents need to be left alone. The answer usually lies within the effectiveness of the provision and/or the parents in meeting the additional needs of the child. Many parents have much to teach the educational, health and social care environments about their child and their individual needs, whereas other parents are, understandably, finding the raising of the child with SEN very difficult.

Some leaders have developed the idea of home–school liaison workers who bridge the gaps between the two settings. They gain an informed understanding of the different environments and also of what strategies can reasonably be implemented in those settings. Ideally, these workers would be jointly funded by Education and Social Care. A number of SEN environments have also provided a range of training and support to parents and carers but it must always be remembered that school is not always the best or most appropriate place to hold the training.

The area of compulsory action may well be a particular issue for those working with pupils with SEBD. As has been identified earlier, these particular youngsters often have parallel difficulties with their families and/or local communities, and it must be recognised that this may well be a case of the parents being unsure as to how to handle their child's behaviour rather than actually condoning it. Herein lies another reason to identify how the state – education, health and social services – can intervene in a positive way to support parents.

Early intervention and effective protection

The actions identified to meet this area are as follows:

- improving information sharing;
- developing a common assessment framework;
- introducing a lead professional; and
- developing on-the-spot service delivery.

The government recognised the need to remove the legislative barriers that inhibit effective information sharing. It also aimed to develop a common assessment framework to ensure that there was a reduction in the need for the duplication of information across a range of services. The document also identifies the idea of introducing a lead professional for those youngsters who have involvement from more than one specialist agency. Professionals are also to be encouraged to work as part of a multi-disciplinary team based in and around the school, and these teams would be able to respond to the concerns of frontline workers.

Possible implications

All leaders welcomed the principles behind improving information sharing and the development of a common assessment framework. Many gave accounts of the frustrations of information being available but not being able to be shared. The co-ordination of this was seen as having a significant resource implication, and this was further exacerbated by the notion of a lead professional. While it was recognised that this, again, was a good idea, the practicalities of making it happen were seen to be a significant challenge. There was a concern that schools would be seen as best placed to provide this role but that there was not the capacity to undertake it, and the same issue existed within social care and health settings. This resource shortfall, be it for financial reasons or just an inability to recruit and retain staff, was also seen as a major stumbling block to the 'encouragement' of 'on-the-spot' multi-disciplinary teams. The language used – 'encouraged' – was also seen as a surefire way of this not being successfully achieved unless significant additional resources were allocated.

Accountability and integration

Some of the areas identified as action points by the government are as follows:

- legislating to create the post of Director of Children's Services;
- legislating to create a lead council member for children;
- developing Children's Trusts; and
- creating an integrated inspection framework for children's services.

The aim of the government is to integrate key services for children and young people under the Director of Children's Services who would report directly to the lead council member, as part of Children's Trusts. These would bring together local authority education, children's social services and some children's health services as well as additional bodies who have a role with children. These trusts are expected to normally report directly to local elected members.

Possible implications

Leaders were in agreement that having someone responsible across the boundaries of education, social services and, hopefully, health was a positive move in attempting to move the 'joined up' agenda forward. Whether this was to become a reality was still to be judged, as in those areas where this had already happened it was still in the very early stages. For leaders in SEN environments it would hopefully lead to a simplification of function as one of the additional challenges is that of managing staff from across a number of sectors. If all these groups ultimately reported to one person this was seen as a positive move. The development of Children's Trusts which reported directly to locally elected members was seen as positive as it gave greater credibility to the role of Director of Children's Services.

The creation of an integrated inspection framework was also seen as positive – those working within residential provision had Ofsted and the Care Standards Framework to work from – and one that had been established in a 'joined-up' way should lead to fewer anomalies.

Workforce reform

The area of workforce reform is one that the current Labour government has expressed a keen desire to move forward throughout the public sector, and this has emanated from the ideas and approaches put forward in *Every Child Matters*; as such, the possible implications for leaders of SEN environments will be covered within this section.

Some of the measures proposed by the government are as follows:

- ensuring effective incentives for good practitioners to stay on the front line;
- high-profile recruitment campaign for entry into children's workforce;
- reducing bureaucracy; and
- a leadership development programme to foster high-quality leadership.

The further development of pay and progression for those teachers reaching the Threshold Standards and the continued Advanced Skills Teacher route are examples of improving incentives to good practitioners to remain as classroom teachers. There continues to be a high-profile campaign to recruit a range of adults into working with children through a range of media. The 'Time for Standards' initiative (2002) is clearly focused on reducing bureaucracy and/or looking at who is best placed to undertake specific tasks. The National College for School Leadership has been given the task of continuing to promote a cohesive approach to leadership development through its 'five stages of leadership' model, ensuring there are leadership programmes for staff at all stages.

Possible implications

The difficulties in implementing movement up the Upper Pay Spine following Threshold has been covered in many books and articles and is not any different in SEN environments than in mainstream settings, other than the difficulties in effectively measuring pupil progress. The Advanced Skills Teacher (AST) route was seen as positive by the majority of leaders of SEN settings as it gave opportunities for excellent practitioners to be rewarded, and it gave them time to share these skills across their own school and in others. The ongoing monitoring of how much AST time was given to other schools was noted as being very variable. It was also noted that some authorities and districts had been more creative with the use of ASTs than others. Some, such as Action Leeds, had created Inclusion ASTs alongside particular curriculum areas, while the post of AST for working with assistants was seen as a very worthwhile post and one in which many teachers from SEN environments were particularly skilled. The unfortunate flipside of creating opportunities and rewards for these staff to remain in the frontline was that many leaders identified a dearth of staff wishing to take on leadership positions.

The 'Time for Standards' agenda and linked workforce reform strategy has been one of the most hotly debated issues for some time. The different teacher unions have had a range of disagreements about elements of it, and implementing the Upper Pay Spine is part of these discussions. The role of support staff in classrooms is the particular area where there has been much debate and discussion with a concern among some that it was a backdoor way of reducing the need for teachers. The leaders from SEN environments felt less threatened by this particular move and welcomed the move to get teachers teaching again, although there were real concerns about the implementation of guaranteed planning and preparation time without additional funding being put in. Many of the leaders stated that many, if not all, of the tasks identified as not requiring a teacher to complete had already been moved to admin or classroom support staff.

It was also noted that the much-lauded development of a career path for support staff (Higher Level Teaching Assistants) was not a reality for those in SEN environments as many had already developed such a career path. Many felt that there were still a number of challenges to be faced if the agreement was to be successfully implemented and that it required additional funding to do this without negatively impacting on pupils.

The final area is that of leadership programmes and their development by NCSL. Leaders felt that there was much to be gained from the different stages of leadership development as identified by NCSL and that in many ways the real challenge lay in attracting younger staff to want to take on leadership positions. A number of the leaders of SEN environments recognised the need for a dual approach to the development of successful leaders within their settings. First, the need to undertake professional development alongside mainstream peers, which was seen as highly beneficial, and secondly, the need for specific professional development pertinent to their setting. Many leaders also noted that to move inclusion forward there was a need to have a stronger element of this within the different professional development packages at the different stages.

The second major initiative to be studied is that of *Removing Barriers to Achievement* (2004). *Removing Barriers to Achievement* sets out the government's vision for giving children with special educational needs and disabilities the opportunity to succeed. It builds on the proposals for the reform of children's services in *Every Child Matters* and also the reform agenda enshrined in law in the SEN and Disability Act 2001.

It proposes to provide clear national leadership, supported by an ambitious programme of sustained action and review, nationally and locally, over a number of years in four key areas:

- Early intervention
- Removing barriers to learning
- Raising expectations and achievement
- Delivering improvements in partnership

These four areas will now be explored in a little more detail, picking out key actions proposed by the government which have particular relevance to those working in SEN environments and the possible implications for SEN environments.

Early intervention

The focus of this is to ensure that children who have difficulties in learning receive the help they need as soon as possible and that parents of children with SEN and disabilities have access to suitable childcare.

In all of the sections it is recognised where the UK currently is with regards to the aims and where it would like to be, and actions that will be taken to get the UK there. Within this section the focus is on implementing pilot projects on a national scale as well as on developing a new strategy for the care of those with SEN and disability which promotes an integrated approach. It talks about working with voluntary organisations on a feasibility study for establishing a National Early Intervention Centre of Excellence. It also states that it will promote further delegation of SEN funding to schools and cut bureaucracy.

Possible implications

Nearly everyone working within any SEN environment will agree that early intervention is the best approach. A number of the leaders identified the desire to be proactive rather than reactive, and this is one such approach. The idea of working with the voluntary sector is a common thread throughout this document and while it was recognised by many leaders that this was a sensible way forward, it was noted by one leader that there needed to be a shared professional understanding as to how the relationship was going to work. It was the experience of a number of the leaders that some people working within the voluntary sector had particular agendas which did not always meet the needs of individual pupils.

Removing barriers to learning

The government aims to do this by embedding inclusive practice in every school and early years setting. Some of the actions it proposes to take in order to achieve this are as follows:

- supporting schools in developing effective inclusive practice through a new Inclusion Development Programme bringing together education, health, social care and the voluntary sector;
- working with the National College for School Leadership to ensure that leadership programmes promote inclusive practice;
- clarifying the future role for special schools:
    strong focus on high standards;
    partnership working with mainstream schools;
    encourage involvement in diversity programmes:
        specialist schools
        leading-edge partnerships
        federations and clusters;
- pump-priming regional centres of excellence for low-incidence SEN;
- producing practical guidance on reducing reliance on high-cost placements in residential special schools; and
- setting minimum standards for SEN advisory and support services.

Possible implications

A common thread throughout the strategy is the development of the 'joined-up' approach, building on the *Every Child Matters* Green Paper. It is an approach that has been espoused by the Labour Government over a number of years and one which those leading and working in SEN environments would dearly like to see happen. *Removing Barriers to Achievement* and *Every Child Matters* are certainly steps in the right direction but the actual direct outcomes from these were still to be felt at school level. It was also felt that the Inclusion Development Programme did not yet have enough detail to know how it was going to impact, if at all.

The idea to promote inclusive practices within leadership programmes was again seen as a positive step, but judgement was deferred until the actual action was seen. All leaders welcomed the idea that there was going to be more clarity regarding the future role of special schools. As has been identified on a number of occasions throughout this book, a major additional challenge for leaders in SEN environments was often the ambiguity regarding their role. The successful leaders had clarity regarding their view of the role of their SEN environment, and the involvement in the diversity programmes identified demonstrated the ability of the highly effective leader to 'invent' the future, as is demonstrated through the case study material. It is also true to say that they were all disappointed by the identification of a strong focus on high standards as this was inherent within all the work they did. It must be noted that the leaders interviewed are not a truly representative group as all were successful leaders, and without the strong focus on high standards they were unlikely to have become successful.

The issue of developing provision for low-incidence SEN and reducing reliance on placement in residential special schools are two areas that could have significant implications both for those working within the maintained and non-maintained/independent sectors. Changing pupil profile within most SEN environments has already been discussed and a number of leaders expressed concern that they would be expected to provide for low-incidence and, usually, more complex pupils without the appropriate support and funding being made available. Where there was recognition of the additional support required there were positive examples of being able to keep pupils within their local community successfully, but all leaders, including those working within the independent sector, felt that very specialised provision occupied a niche within the continuum of SEN provision and that this would continue.

The final area identified within this section is that of setting minimum standards for SEN advisory and support services. All leaders welcomed this and many felt that these should be located within the SEN environment, with a number of SEN settings already providing this, often through self-funding.

Raising expectations and achievement

This would be achieved by developing teachers' skills and strategies for meeting the needs of children with SEN and by sharpening the focus on the progress made by children with SEN. Some of the actions identified are:

- develop practical teaching and learning resources;
- ensure that Initial Teacher Training (ITT) provides good grounding in core skills and knowledge of SEN;
- promote and extend the use of P-scales and collect data nationally from 2005;
- consult on changes to performance tables;
- improve transition planning;
- improve educational and training opportunities post-school.

Possible implications

The development of practical teaching and learning resources would be welcomed by all the leaders but most were highly sceptical as to whether this would be achieved. All national strategies had, eventually, attempted to produce resources for those working with pupils with SEN, but these were of very little use within the more specialised SEN environments. Many stated that a better idea would be to devolve funding to enable networks of SEN environments to develop these materials themselves.

The issue regarding ITT has been covered in more detail in Chapter 5. Suffice to say that this proposal was welcomed, but a number of leaders articulated a wish that it could have gone further and identified the role of SEN environments in assisting HE providers in the delivery of SEN training, and also that it was compulsory within all teacher-training courses, and not an optional module as was currently the case with many courses.

The use of P-scales within SEN environments was now widespread and leaders saw this further development as a clear role for their settings in assisting mainstream teachers to use P-scales effectively. There was still a need to develop supporting tools and methods of moderation. With regard to the collection of data nationally from 2005, successful SEN environments had been doing this for a number of years and it was hoped that their experiences and knowledge would be drawn upon. The case study of Addington School's attempt to make meaningful use of the data demonstrates the complexities that remain, and therefore the use of P-scales needs to be carefully developed. The inclusion of the achievements of pupils with SEN within league tables was also welcomed although the abolition of league tables, as unlikely as this was, was identified as being a major factor in further developing an inclusive educational environment.

Much work had been done by a number of the successful leaders in attempting to assist in the development of co-ordinated and joined-up transition plans for pupils with SEN, and the development of national standards for health and social care was welcomed as a positive step. Earlier case study material demonstrates Blackfriars School head teacher Clive Lilley's approach to developing post-school provision, namely the development of such provision itself.

Delivering improvements in partnership

The government aims to achieve this by taking a hands-on approach to improvement so that parents can be confident that their child will get the education they need. Some actions they identify that will be taken are as follows:

- make inclusion an integral part of school self-evaluation and Ofsted to judge this; and for data to be published in performance tables;

- further development of the SEN National Performance Framework;
- build on proposals from *Every Child Matters*.

Possible implications

Inclusion is already built into an Ofsted inspection and the report has a separate section detailing inspectors' findings. This was viewed as a positive action as all schools, whether really wishing to be inclusive or not, are keen to get a good, or better, Ofsted inspection report. The ramifications of this had already been felt by some leaders where mainstream leaders had directly approached them for support in demonstrating their inclusiveness. The further use of inclusion kitemarks, such as the Inclusion Quality mark developed by Caroline Coles and Robert Hancock, was also seen as positive as it raised the status of inclusion.

The publishing of data on inclusiveness was seen as a real mixed blessing. While it raised the status of inclusion it could also be seen as a negative for a number of schools and their stakeholders if this was impacting on their status within the league tables on attainment. A much more effective method of promoting inclusion was to include this factor within the attainment league tables and therefore those who were inclusive and achieved good results would appear near the top, as opposed to schools that may be discriminatory in their approaches in the pursuance of high league table status. A number of leaders also noted that many mainstream leaders expressed concerns regarding being seen as good with pupils with SEN as this led to more parents of pupils with SEN wishing to attend their school in preference to the local school.

The possible implications of the SEN National Performance Framework were still not possible to identify at the current stage of development and the proposals of *Every Child Matters* are covered earlier in this chapter.

The statement of Charles Clarke, then Secretary of State for Education and Skills, within his foreword to the document – 'All children, wherever they are educated, need to be able to learn, play and develop alongside each other within their local community of schools' – signals a shift away from the shutting of all SEN environments which many feared with the rise of the inclusion debate. The document identifies what it sees as the future of special schools as providing education for children with the most severe and complex needs and sharing their specialist skills and knowledge to support inclusion in mainstream schools.

Leaders from all SEN environments were, on the whole, pleased with the language, tone and possible implications of *Removing Barriers to Achievement*, but as one leader put it, 'At the moment this is philosophically a breath of fresh air, but if nothing changes then rhetoric is all it will have been'. Perhaps the document itself most clearly identifies its success criteria when stating that the success in achieving the vision must be reflected in the way we:

- train our teachers;
- fund our schools; and
- judge their achievements.

Only time will tell as to whether there has been a significant enough 'sea-change' to say that the government has been successful in removing barriers to achievement, or at least reducing them.

Summary

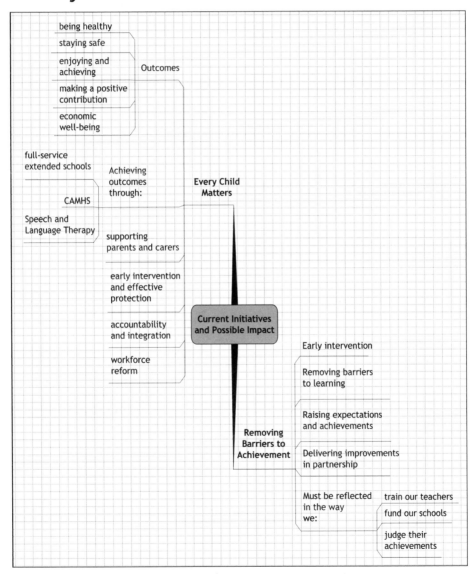

Figure 6.2 Current Initiatives and Possible Impact summary

The leader of SEN in the future

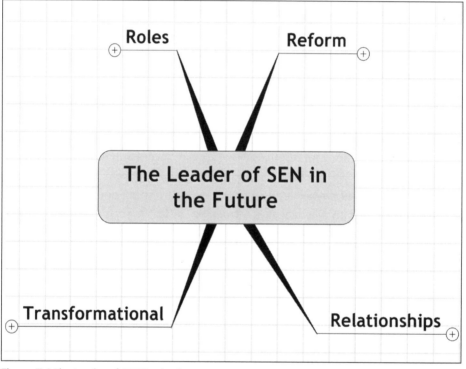

Figure 7.1 The Leader of SEN in the Future

> There are three categories of people: the ones that make things happen; the ones that watch things happen; and the ones that wonder what the hell is happening.
>
> (Prashnig 1998)

This chapter certainly does not aim to produce an 'identikit' leader of SEN in the future, as what has become crystal clear from the discussions and interviews with successful leaders in a range of SEN environments is that there is no perfect model to which a prospective leader of SEN can aspire. What is clear is that there is a range of skills and qualities that ensure that the successful SEN leader in the future is someone who falls into the first category of people identified above. A number of the areas identified are not specific to leaders of SEN but remain relevant as many leadership issues are common across all settings.

One element that is needed in order to redefine what role special education plays in an increasingly changing education system, and to allow for the innovation described earlier, is the need to engage in the systematic abandonment of old ways including:

- design – abandonment of previously held models;
- boundary spanning – abandonment of 'silo' model and belief that problems and solutions occur in one simple sector;
- curriculum – abandonment of many carefully built-up curriculum areas in order to introduce and establish new areas; and
- pedagogy – abandonment of old styles in favour of the new knowledge of learning styles.

The leader of SEN in the future is one who will question the *status quo* – if you don't question it then you will not change it. The ability and desire to ask questions about what is being done and why, and to challenge long-held assumptions, was a common feature of those successful leaders who were interviewed.

When a leader and his/her setting embark on a sustained period of reform there are undoubtedly many challenges that will be faced. In such a period of rapid change the need for moral leadership will be a prerequisite for a successful leader and this needs to be based on a firm set of personal values which will include: integrity; social justice; humanity; respect; loyalty; and sharp distinction between right and wrong.

Strategic relationships will not be successfully initiated, developed and maintained if such a value system is not strongly held and exercised on a regular and consistent basis.

The major challenges that lie ahead will not be achieved by direct conflict, although the need to be authoritative in leadership style at each major change was identified by more than one successful leader. The ability to resolve conflict will be a key quality of the successful leader of SEN in the future. The need to bring about the necessary changes and to challenge some of the long-held beliefs will not meet with success if the leader does not display inner strength and courage.

The importance of strategy will remain, but it is through relationships and not plans that it will be exercised. Even the typical three-year plan, with 12 months firm and two years draft, cannot survive in an age of uncertainty. It is the nature and quality of the leader's relationships, both internal and external, that will be crucial to the success of the school.

Developing effective relationships will be achieved through:

- development of trust;
- open communication;
- making meaning work;
- empowerment of individuals and teams; and
- development of teams through involvement.

The successful leader of SEN in the future will be effective in building extended communities both within their setting and also with the wider community. That will undoubtedly be with other schools and with other agencies, but it will also include some agencies or stakeholders with whom there would not have been a relationship in previous times. The ability to harness the will and skills of a diverse and expanding group of partners, both within and outside the complex organisation which is a school or service, is crucial in ensuring that the SEN setting is led successfully and meets the needs and aspirations of all stakeholders. During such a period of discontinuous and accelerating change tomorrow's leaders need to embrace change with optimism and with the conviction that resistance can be overcome and that differences can be reconciled. It must also be acknowledged that there is the need to build a learning community with a high level of intelligence. This involves the need to build a broader set of basics such as:

- systems thinking;
- the ability to utilise technology in learning;
- working co-operatively in high-performing teams which may change depending on the project;
- taking the initiative; and
- the ability to acquire new skills.

These learning communities will operate within the SEN environment and across the partnerships that have been developed. The leader of SEN in the future needs to foster these skills within his/her own setting.

Peter Upton (2002) identifies what he calls the six Cs for school leadership:

- Compelling vision
- Collaboration
- Critical friends
- Culture of development

- Congruence
- Clear focus

The ability to foster a shared vision is a key component in being a successful leader. In the past, vision was often thought to be sufficient in itself, but this is no longer the case. Successful leaders of SEN are able to share the vision with different groups of people in different ways, and as one leader identified, stakeholders need to have confidence in their leader as having 'got the map'. One leader identified the need to be aware of the 'Marks & Spencer factor', i.e. the need to constantly guard against complacency and the need to think big and imagine the impossible. This requires passion in addition to vision. Radical solutions must become the norm if current and future aspirations are to be met. Dramatic organisational change can occur within a system if driven by passion and commitment.

The area of collaboration has been much discussed throughout this book and as such needs no further discussion here. The idea of critical friends is one often used when describing the role of governors within schools. While undoubtedly those governing bodies that are very effective do undertake this role successfully, there are many situations where the governors, despite their best intentions, struggle to fulfil this role. The effective leader actively seeks out people to act in the critical friend role, both within the school and outside, to ensure ideas and approaches have been thoroughly explored.

A number of the leaders interviewed expressed a grave concern regarding the future recruitment of leaders within their SEN environments, and therefore, as identified by one leader, they felt they needed to do more within their own service to promote leadership development. The NCSL have encouraged much discussion on distributed or dispersed leadership and successful leaders have actively sought to develop this within their school communities.

The final two areas identified by Upton – congruence and clear focus – are closely linked. The leader of SEN, now and in the future, needs to ensure that in spite of the myriad initiatives and sometimes competing agendas, they develop congruence for those within their setting and keep a clear focus on what they want to achieve, and are not diverted too far from the path.

> If schools are to be that different, there will be a radical shift in the challenges faced by their leaders and in the qualities needed for such a role.
>
> (Bennett 2000)

Throughout the discussions with successful leaders and from reading current literature, the use of different leadership styles was a common theme. A number of the leaders identified the need to be able to adopt different leadership styles depending on what was required in a particular situation. They identified the need to move back to an authoritative style at each major change but then be able to move to the coaching style as soon as possible. What became clear from the discussions and from reading was that the concept of transformational leadership will be the style of leadership required from the leader of SEN in the future.

Transformational leadership, as identified by LRDL (2004), is based on integrity, openness and transparency. It recognises, values and promotes the talents of each individual within an organisation. It articulates a shared vision that empowers employees through developing potential. It not only enables settings to cope with change but it also enables them to be proactive in determining the change. Transformational leadership is also proactive in nurturing leadership within all individuals. Clearly, this is the leadership style that is required now and in the future in order for leaders of SEN to be successful and build successful schools and services.

As identified by Clarke and Cohn, in Caldwell (2002), there are three essential elements to the transformational reform: restructuring, reorganising and re-culturing.

Restructuring includes looking again at learning and teaching practices and at the policies and procedures that govern the school; *reorganising* includes looking at the roles of leaders and staff within schools, the size and purpose of schools and how the school is measured; *re-culturing* is looking at the beliefs, values and assumptions that shape the behaviour of members of the school community. For the leader of SEN in the future to be successful they need to engage in all three elements if they are to bring about transformational reform within their settings.

Brighouse (2002) identifies five roles that successful leaders will need to adopt:

- learner
- historian and futurologist
- pogo-stick player
- climate setter
- utility player

The leader of SEN in the future needs to ensure that their knowledge is up to date and that they model the learning they would want from their staff. The role of historian and futurologist is always to be looking at ways to invent the future while keeping a keen eye on the past to ensure the same mistakes are not made again. The role of pogo-stick player is having the ability to keep the overview needed to be a successful leader while ensuring that your feet spend some time on the ground, understanding the implications of strategic decisions that have been made. Climate setting is ensuring that you always remain positive and that you reward staff for the successful implementation of changes, and saying (and meaning) 'thankyou' for their day-to-day achievements in what are often stressful environments. The final role identified by Brighouse, that of utility player, has at least two meanings. First, there is the role within school, the ability to interact, talk and work with the full range of staff in a meaningful and appropriate way; and secondly, there is the ability to interact, talk and work with the full range of external people, be they politicians, other head teachers or senior staff from other professions.

For leaders of mainstream environments wishing to develop their settings to be more inclusive, the work by Kugelmass (2003) identified common characteristics shared by leaders of inclusive mainstream schools in the UK, USA and Portugal as follows:

- uncompromising commitment to inclusive education;
- clearly defined roles, responsibilities and boundaries;
- collaborative interpersonal style;
- problem-solving and conflict-resolution skills;
- understanding and appreciation of the expertise of others; and
- supportive relationships with other staff.

Identified below are a number of key skills and abilities shared by current successful leaders of SEN environments. Some of these add further credibility to the topics already covered within this chapter while some help to further clarify the skills and practices that will need to be used by the future leader of SEN:

- sharing the vision but being very clear that change is needed;
- ability to communicate the vision and bring people on board;
- creating a culture of openness;
- shared decision-making;
- creating the best structure for change;
- leading by example – do not ask staff to do something you are not prepared to do yourself;
- being alert to what is expected – grasping the initiative;
- looking always to develop the capabilities of individuals;
- non-protectionist.

The case study material contained within this book gives many examples of the ways that many successful leaders of SEN environments are demonstrating these skills in practice.

> I believe that schools are lighthouses. I believe that every school harbors within its wall the capacity for grown-ups and students to become inventors and reformers to engage in authentic change.
>
> (Barth 2001)

Summary

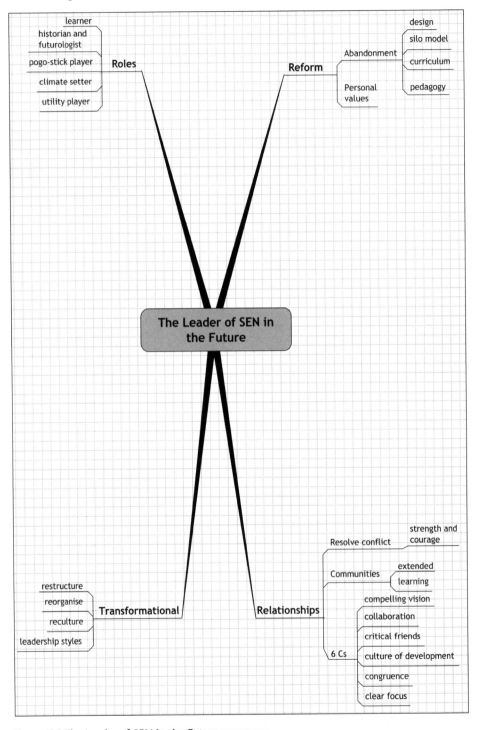

Figure 7.2 The Leader of SEN in the Future summary

SEN provision of the future

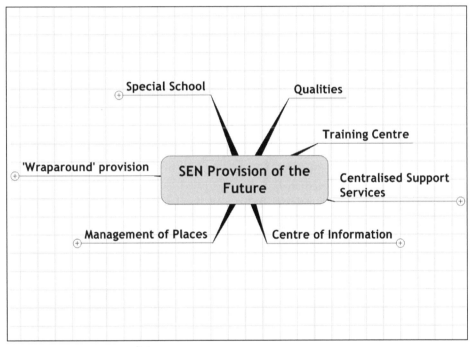

Figure 8.1 SEN Provision of the Future

> It is time to look beyond what we are used to, what is familiar to us and what has
> worked in the past. Only then will we be able to cope with the demands of the future
> and actually enjoy the change process.
>
> (Prashnig 1998)

As with the chapter on 'The leader of SEN in the future', this chapter is not an
attempt to produce an identikit for the 'perfect' SEN provision of the future as the
continuum of need provided by the SEN environments visited in preparation for

the writing of this book is immense. What it aims to do is to draw some common factors that I believe are necessary for the SEN provision of the future, while acknowledging that there will be contextual factors that mean that variations are a necessity. Case study material provided throughout the book demonstrates how some SEN environments are already 'living in the future'.

From discussions, observations and reading it appears that the SEN provision of the future will have the following qualities as learning organisations. They will:

- see diversity as the new reality;
- tailor learning individually;
- use collaborative teaching arrangements;
- collaborate with families, agencies and other community members;
- be organised and structured flexibly;
- have high expectations of success;
- build inclusive learning communities; and
- keep improving.

Seeing diversity as the new reality means that the SEN provisions must recognise that not only must they meet the needs of a wider range of pupils but that also this must include a knowledge of individual learning styles and the fact that one curriculum will not meet the needs of all pupils. It is also slowly being recognised that pupils learn in lots of different places and in lots of different ways. The SEN provisions of the future will need to ensure they use different strategies and approaches that personalise learning according to the individuals' learning abilities, needs, styles, purposes and preferences. With this as the new reality, teachers and other staff with different areas of expertise and skill will need to work together in order individually to tailor learning to better meet the needs of the pupils.

Enhanced collaboration with health and social services will lead to SEN provision being more effective, comprehensive and supportive of pupils' lives. Increasing and improving links with the wider community is another way that SEN provision resources can be enriched and extended. For those non-residential settings this will mean establishing closer links with respite provision to ensure an holistic approach to meeting the needs of pupils with SEN. It also means working with health and social services in attempting to establish a more co-ordinated, fairer approach to the distribution of support, such as the development of a health matrix of need as developed by Action Leeds with their counterparts in Health.

SEN provision of the future will be organised in ways that are adaptable to the needs of the pupils and teachers. Innovative timetables, school teams and working times can all offer opportunities for educators to respond flexibly to pupil differences and, therefore, be able to respond to needs beyond the current school day and school year.

SEN provision of the future will be at the forefront of building inclusive communities. These settings should lead on demonstrating how individual differences are valued and celebrated within the local and wider community. These provisions will lead in the collection and use of meaningful information for parents, teachers, students and policy-makers to enable continued improvement for pupils with SEN.

For the inclusive mainstream environment of the future there appears to be a need to develop the following cultural characteristics as identified by Kugelmass (2003):

- initial motivation for inclusion supported by external forces;
- uncompromising commitment and belief in inclusive education;
- differences among students and staff perceived as a resource;
- teaming and a collaborative interactional style among staff and children;
- willingness to struggle to sustain practices;
- inclusion understood as a social/political issue; and
- symbolism (visual and linguistic) – communicated ideals and spread commitments across the school and community.

> Special schools need to be confident, outward looking centres of excellence.
> (DfES 'Programme of Action' Meeting Special Education Needs 2001)

So what roles will the outward-looking centre of excellence in SEN provision of the future play? It is highly likely that the roles will be many and varied depending on the particular circumstances of that setting. A number of these possible roles are now explored.

Many SEN provisions of the future will be seen as training centres which provide training and assessment opportunities leading to recognised accreditation for:

- support staff;
- teachers; and
- mainstream colleagues.

See the case study on Addington School's development as an NVQ Training and Assessment Centre.

As SEN environments contain a high level of knowledge and expertise it would make sense if they were the base for a centralised support services arrangement. A number of leading SEN environments already provide this service, either formally or informally, and putting together all support services into a small number of SEN provisions means that there can be the development of an ongoing and joined-up approach to support arrangements built between the different services. This will need the further development of Service Level Agreements which are the more formal arrangements that will need to be put into place between the SEN provision and mainstream partners and/or the LEA or other partners. This more formal agreement will be required to ensure that partnerships that are established are not lost when key players move on. The case study material on Blackfriars gives such an example.

SEN provision of the future will also be seen, and work, as a centre of information. Most SEN settings, as previously recognised, are a significant resource in terms of specialist knowledge, and the management of this needs to be recognised and further developed. The following areas show some of the possibilities that are achievable by the SEN setting being seen as and working as a centre of information:

- enabling greater access for pupils with special needs within mainstream settings by providing assessment and advice regarding the use of ICT and curriculum access needs;
- identifying need – the development of special schools as assessment centres where pupils may come to have needs assessed prior to attending the most appropriate educational establishment;
- providing support to:
  other professionals who work with individuals with special needs to enable their delivery to become more effective through SEN awareness and/or training;
  parents – this has been mentioned in a number of places throughout this book. All SEN provisions have an extremely important role to play with parents in terms of developing greater support for them and also facilitating support groups for parents. These can take the form of training in some areas to help support the parents but, as has been noted elsewhere, care and thought must be given to the location of the training;
  other schools through the provision of outreach. Although this is already established in many SEN provisions, their development needs to be continued to ensure there are more formal agreements with LEAs and/or individual schools;
- resources – a significant level of specialised resource lies within many SEN provisions and the use of this to aid access and support pupils with SEN in mainstream provision needs to be further developed.

Although many leaders of SEN provision have given support, advice and training for minimal or, often, no cost, the future SEN provision will need to become more adept and proficient at selling services. Although many of the areas identified as part of this section have been provided within current special school or LEA resources, it has to be acknowledged that with the increasing delegation to schools these may have to be purchased. As case study material on the development of Blackfriars as a Key Learning Centre, and Crosshills Technology College, shows, effective and successful leaders of these SEN provisions have used this additional funding to further develop their capacity to successfully meet the needs of a wider range of pupils with SEN. The development of SEN provision as centres of information is further identified in the Action Leeds initiative of developing their special schools as Specialist Inclusive Learning Centres.

Increasingly, SEN provisions will become gateways to networked provision for individuals. As this develops, the management of places, including dual-role placement, means that the greater flexibility of placement needs to be recognised and the need for careful management arises to ensure that the pupil receives the educational provision that best meets his/her needs. An important new role in assisting in this development may be the development of the keyworker role used in many residential establishments. This keyworker will usually not be a teacher but will have a good understanding of the range of educational provisions available, and will, where necessary, act as advocate for the individual and broker the most effective provision for him/her.

As has been mentioned throughout this book, the need for a joined-up approach will be a continued need for the foreseeable future. The keyworker approach as part of the SEN provision of the future will lead in the development of a 'wraparound' provision for the individual with SEN and his/her family, including, where needed, input and resources from education, health and social care or family and community services.

From reading widely around the subject of the school of the future, as well as having the wonderful opportunity of visiting a range of SEN provisions in the UK and Australia, and talking to many successful and highly effective leaders, the following is an attempt to describe a possible model of SEN provision of the future. As was noted at the start of this chapter, this model comes with a significant health warning, as the continuum of need discussed within this book is necessarily wide and, as such, this model is particularly focused on special schools that cater for those pupils with learning difficulties. For those SEN environments that cater for those with social, emotional and behavioural difficulties there will be much in common, but due to their particular circumstances there may well need to be some differences.

As has also been mentioned previously the development of an appropriate model also depends on current context but there are areas that should stimulate discussion within all SEN provisions. With this in mind the model is as follows:

- main sites that are located near to or on mainstream sites that are relevant to all age groups that the special school is serving;
- a number of satellite classes within mainstream schools that have a separate class base for the times when it is not appropriate or suitable for the pupils with special needs to be in the mainstream class. Also, opportunities for team teaching to take place either in the separate class base or within the mainstream class, including pupils with special needs.

Although a number of leaders believed inclusion was achievable and that there should, in future, not be a need for segregated provision, the model described here is seen as a step towards inclusion, and for the foreseeable future there still needs to be a specialist base for a number of reasons:

- it is important for teachers to have a shared opportunity to develop and foster the necessary skills needed to become more inclusive;
- there is a significant number of pupils who, through their particularly complex needs and/or challenging behaviour, still need the specialist setting;
- although it would be nice for finance not to be a factor, it would be naïve not to recognise it; therefore, it is much more cost-effective to have the specialist resources needed by pupils within one setting; and
- many of the roles identified earlier need a significant base.

The idea of having satellite classes, within the role of the special school, is for the following reasons:

- to enable a much greater flexibility of provision than is currently available in many areas;
- to enable the mixing of mainstream and special school staff and the sharing of good practice;
- ongoing opportunities for professional development for mainstream and special school staff to build schools that are more inclusive and able to meet a wider range of pupil need successfully;
- to 'protect' the mainstream school from the inclusion of more pupils with special needs skewing their placing in the league tables – another factor which it would be nice, but currently naïve, to ignore.

The concept of federations of schools, where there are formal agreements between schools, seems to be the most secure way of building on personal relationships between leaders to ensure long-term commitment. Ideally, this would be developed alongside partnerships with health and social services to provide an holistic service provision to pupils with special needs, one which is co-funded by all.

The nearest models to the one described above, that are in current operation and have been seen by the author, are in Oxfordshire and Perth, Australia.

Oxfordshire has a number of special schools that have adopted a co-location approach to their development. Bishopswood, in Sonning, is co-located within the local primary and secondary schools. A number of other special schools have classes within mainstream schools that remain under the role of the special school.

In Western Australia there is a range of provisions:

- Education Support School – led by a Principal and very similar to the UK's separate special schools;
- Education Support Centre – again led by a Principal, but this time the centre is located within a mainstream school;
- Education Support Unit – this is run by a Team Leader (head of department) within a mainstream school under the direction of the mainstream principal.

In order to provide an appropriate continuum of provision to meet the range of need required for pupils with SEN, the SEN provision of the future would, in the author's view, provide the full range of options identified from Western Australia but under the direction of one leader. The main reason for this is that, given the correct systems and a structure being put in place, if a wide range of provision is available under one leader, then it is much less likely that the barriers that currently exist in being able to meet individual needs appropriately and flexibly will exist. The time, energy and expense that often currently meet the desire to move a child from special to mainstream, or vice versa, will be greatly reduced if a more flexible SEN provision is developed, given that it is led by the effective and successful leader of SEN described earlier.

The best way to predict the future is to invent it.

(Alan Kay, in Dryden and Vos 2000)

Summary

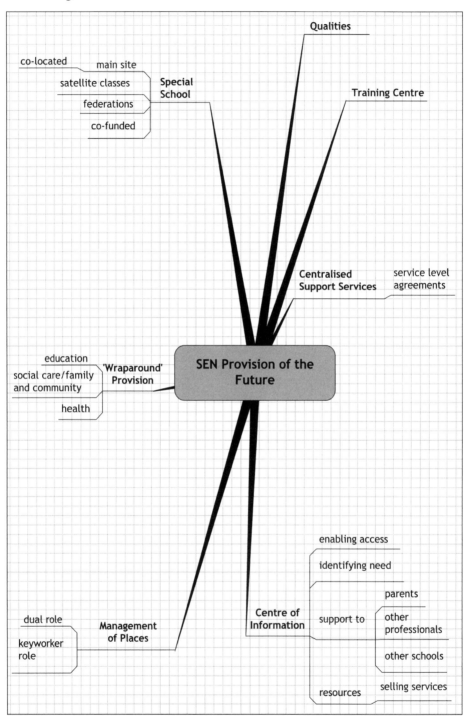

Figure 8.2 SEN Provision of the Future summary

References and further reading

Abbott, J. (1997) *The Child Is Father of the Man.* Stafford: Network Educational Press.

Abbott, J. (1999) *The 21st Century Learning Initiative.* Stafford: Network Educational Press.

Ainscow, M. (2000) 'Developing inclusive schools: implications for leadership'. NCSL essay, May.

Allen, B. (2003) *Changing Minds: The Psychology of Managing Challenging Behaviour within an Ethical and Legal Framework.* St Leonards-on-Sea: Steaming Publishing.

Barth, R. (2001) *Learning by Heart.* San Francisco, CA: Jossey Bass.

Bayliss, V. (2000) 'What should our children learn?' *RSA Journal,* December (www.rsa.org.uk).

Bayliss, V. (2001) 'Opening minds, increasing opportunities'. RSA lecture, November (www.rsa.org.uk).

Beare, H. (1996) *Trends for Global Citizenship, for the World of Work, and for Personal Formation.* Jolimont, VA: IARTV.

BECTa (2002) 'Transforming management'. Leadership Pack. Coventry: BECTa.

Bennett, D. (2000) 'The school of the future: key issues for school leaders'. NCSL essay.

Brighouse, T. (2000) 'The new teachers'. RSA lecture, March (www.rsa.org.uk).

Brighouse, T. (2002) 'Doomed to succeed: the *El Dorado* of school leadership'. *Leading Edge,* 5(2).

Burnett, N. (2002) 'Special leadership'. Research Associate Report. Nottingham: NCSL (www.ncsl.org.uk).

Burrows, D. (2001) 'Stevenson: progress and prospects'. *Educate.IT,* 1(3).

Caldwell, B. (2002) 'A blueprint for leadership for the successful transformation of schools in the 21st century'. Paper presented at a seminar, April.

Clarke, L. and Kohn, L. (2002) 'One size doesn't fit all'. Principal leadership article, Vol. 2, no. 6, February, USA.

Cliffen, S. (2002) 'Emotional and behavioural difficulties: some reflections, ideas and perspectives', in Gabbitas Educational Consultants *Schools for Special Needs: A Complete Guide* (10th edn). London: Kogan Page.

Cole, T., Visser, J. and Upton, G. (1998) *Effective Schooling for Pupils with Emotional and Behavioural Difficulties.* London: David Fulton.

Collarbone, P. (2000) *Growing Leaders: The National Agenda for Developing Leadership.* North of England Education Conference.

Corbett, J. (2002) 'Inclusion'. *Special Children*, April.

DFE (1994) *The Education of Children with Emotional and Behavioural Difficulties.* London: Department for Education.

DfES (2001) *Programme of Action: Meeting Special Education Needs.* London: DfES.

DfES (2002a) *Time for Standards: Reforming the School Workforce.* London: DfES.

DfES (2002b) 'Transforming the way we learn'. Discussion document. London: DfES.

DfES (2003a) *Every Child Matters.* London: DfES.

DfES (2003b) *Report of the Special Schools Working Group.* London: DfES.

DfES (2004) *Removing Barriers to Achievement.* London: DfES.

DfES 'Schools of the future'. *Pilot Projects and Information.* DfES website (www.dfes.gov.uk).

Dryden, G. and Vos, J. (2000) *The Learning Revolution.* Auckland, NZ: The Learning Revolution Co.

Fullan, M. (2001) *Leading in a Culture of Change.* San Francisco, CA: Jossey Bass.

Goldberg, M. F. 'Leadership in education: five commonalities' (www.pdkintl.org/kappan/k0106gol.htm).

Green, H. (2002) 'The paradoxes of leadership'. *School Leadership*, Spring.

Hargreaves, A., Shaw, P. and Fink, D. *et al.* (2000) *Change Frames: Supporting Secondary Teachers in Interpreting and Integrating Secondary School Reform.* Toronto: Ontario Institute for the Studies of Education/University of Toronto.

Hargreaves, D. (2002) 'A future for the school curriculum'. Speech on QCA website (www.qca.org.uk/ca/14-19/dh_speech.asp).

Honey, P. (2001) 'The role of e-learning in today's world'. RSA lecture, March (www.rsa.org.uk).

Kugelmass, J.W. (2003) 'Inclusive leadership: leadership for inclusion'. Research Associates Report (www.ncsl.org.uk/).

Leadbeater, C. (2004) *Learning about Personalisation: How Can We Put the Learner at the Heart of the Education System?* DfES/0419/2004. London: DfES.

Leadership Research and Development Ltd (LRDL) (2004) *Identify and Develop Your Leaders: Uncovering the True Nature of Leadership.* LRDL promotional brochure.

McDermott, S. (2002) *How to Be a Complete and Utter Failure in Life, Work and Everything.* Harlow: Pearson Education.

National College for School Leadership (NCSL) (2001) *Leadership Development Framework*. Nottingham: National College for School Leadership.

National Institute for Urban School Improvement (2000a) 'Improving education: the promise of inclusive schooling', USA (www.edc.org/urban/).

National Institute for Urban School Improvement (2000b) 'On preparing teachers for the future', USA (www.edc.org/urban/).

National Institute for Urban School Improvement (2000c) 'On working together', USA (www.edc.org/urban/).

Ofsted (1999) *Principles into Practice: Effective Education for Pupils with Emotional and Behavioural Difficulties*. London: Ofsted.

Peters, T. (2003) *Reimagine*. New York: Dorling Kindersley.

Pijl, S.J. and Dyson, A. (1998) 'Funding special education: a three-country study of demand-oriented models'. *Comparative Education*, **34**(3), 261–79.

Pijl, Y.J. and Pijl, S.J. (1998) 'Are pupils in special education too "special" for regular education?' *European Journal of Special Education*, **44**(1).

Prashnig, B. (1998) *The Power of Diversity*. New Zealand: David Bateman.

Richardson, T. (2002) 'Leadership online'. *Managing Schools Today*, January.

Rodriguez, J.C. and Romaneck, G.M. (2001) 'The practice of inclusion'. *Principal Leadership*, **2**(8).

Stoll, L. (2002) 'Leading for change: building capacity for learning'. *Leading Edge*, **5**(2). London: The London Leadership Centre, University of London Institute of Education.

Stoll, L., Fink, D. and Earl, L. (2004) *It's About Learning (and It's About Time)*. London: RoutledgeFalmer.

SWALSS (2002) 'Special school of the future'. Conference feedback from discussion groups.

Swerdlik M.E., Reeder, G.D. and Bucy, J.E. (1999) 'Full service schools'. *NASSP Bulletin*, November.

Upton, P. (2002) 'International dimensions for the development of school leaders'. *Leading Edge*, **5**(2). London. The London Leadership Centre, University of London Institute of Education.

Index